CATHOLIC FAITH
in a
PROCESS PERSPECTIVE

CATHOLIC FAITH
in a
PROCESS
PERSPECTIVE

Norman Pittenger

ORBIS BOOKS
Maryknoll, New York 10545

The Catholic Foreign Mission Society of America (Maryknoll) recruits and trains people for overseas missionary service. Through Orbis Books Maryknoll aims to foster the international dialogue that is essential to mission. The books published, however, reflect the opinions of their authors and are not meant to represent the official position of the society.

Copyright © 1981 Orbis Books, Maryknoll, NY 10545
All rights reserved
Manufactured in the United States of America

Library of Congress Cataloging in Publication Data

Pittenger, W. Norman (William Norman), 1905-
    Catholic faith in a process perspective.

    Index: p.
    1. Theology, Doctrinal. 2. Process theology.
I. Title.
BT75.2.P57   230'.2   81-9615
ISBN 0-88344-091-1 (pbk.)   AACR2

For
Dorothy Hartshorne,
with great affection

Contents

Preface

For a great many years I have given most of my time and effort to the task of presenting process theology as the best available conceptuality today for the statement of the historic Christian and Catholic faith. Its value has become increasingly clear to me, not least because I am convinced that it comes as close to the truth of things secularly speaking as we in our time are likely to get, while it is also appropriate for the biblical witness to God and God's activity in creation, and invites and demands human action in response.

In furthering this task I have written a number of books; I have also spoken at many universities, theological colleges, and conferences both in Britain and in North America. A considerable number of those places has been associated with the Roman Catholic Church, most recently St. John's University in Collegeville, Minnesota, U.S.A. On these various occasions I have been requested to discuss the way in which the process position approaches religious affirmations and how it differs from the "death of God" movement which was much discussed a decade or more ago; how a process thinker approaches religious faith; what is meant by the "reconception" of that faith; how Whitehead's concept of God is to be interpreted; the way in which a process theologian will look at the facts of evil and suffering; the place of Jesus Christ in this kind of theology, above all with reference to recent consideration of the "incarnation" as mythological statement; what a process thinker can say about the practice of prayer; the meaning of Church and ordained ministry in this perspective; and the question of human liberation from injustice and despotic control, a matter so much in view in the present time. This basic material is collected here and I conclude with an essay on Whitehead and Catholicism.

Since the material in this book is developed from those lectures and addresses, I have not tried to remove all duplication of idea, as that would have meant a serious modification of the argument as it is developed in the treatment of each specific topic. But I do not think that there is any meaningless repetition or reiteration; rather, as it seems to me, there is a viewing of the given subjects from the process slant, but always with the difference that a particular subject requires both in approach and statement.

I will not give here a complete list of the institutions which have invited me to address them. That would be tedious and unnecessary, not least because some of the material has been given in several such places; but I must mention Maryknoll, John Carroll University, Xavier University in Cincinnati, Aquinas Institute in Dubuque, the University of Dayton, Mt. St. Mary's in Baltimore, and the Jesuit House of Studies in Berkeley, among others. I also express my thanks to my many hosts and above all to St. John's University where I spent a happy few weeks during its summer session in 1980, delivering some of the present material.

This book is dedicated to Mrs. Charles Hartshorne, without asking her consent since I am sure that her modesty and continuing self-effacement would have brought a "No" to any such suggestion. Dorothy Hartshorne is a "beautiful person," to use a phrase popular with younger people today. Not only is she the devoted wife of Charles Hartshorne, for so many years my friend and mentor; she is also his faithful fellow-worker, quite as much as a distinguished authority (in her own right) on Japanese culture and art. Their home in Austin, Texas, is a lovely place, where friends and other guests are always welcome and where anyone who visits them is aware of a loving care which surely is a manifestation of the divine charity. If a basic metaphysic ought to reflect itself in human behavior, the insistence that God is sheer Love in act, upon which Charles Hartshorne has written and spoken so much and always with the help and support of his wife, is vividly and compellingly expressed in the Hartshornes' generosity, unfailing kindness, and gracious hospitality.

1

Toward Understanding
Religious Affirmations

Deep in human existence, despite our often superficial attitudes
and our momentary feelings of frustration and senselessness,
there is a feeling that life is worth living, that somehow it has a
meaning, and that we "count" in the world. Of course I am aware
of the fact that all of us have our times of "quiet desperation," in
Thoreau's phrase. I am not suggesting for a moment that human
living is inevitably a bright and cheerful affair. I do not accept the
notion that we are to be starry-eyed optimists who minimize or
even deny the dark side of experience. What I am saying is that in
the enterprise of our human living there is an often unconscious
acceptance of the value or worth of that living. But if this is the
case, then we must enquire into the implications of that sense of
worth.

In my view, that sense must somehow or other be "grounded"
in the nature of things. I put it thus vaguely because it would be
absurd to proceed, for example, to a theistic faith without further
consideration of such matters as our observation of how things go
in the world, without due recognition of the questions which any
talk about how things observably go must inevitably raise. But I
believe that we can say that the very fact of the sense of worth for
human existence is associated with the rational, emotional,
conational, and (often forgotten in this context) aesthetic aspects
of our total experience. The sense of worth, profoundly if inartic-
ulately felt by each one of us, is tied in with how we think, how
we feel, how we strive, and how we appreciate. And if this is true,
then it would seem to follow that any attempt to make sense of the

ways in which that feeling of worth articulates or expresses itself in concrete human life must take into account what these aspects have to tell us, as they get themselves worked out in actual religious patterns.

For such patterns *do* exist. The religious side of our experience is too persistent and is found in too many places and among too many people of most varied types and races and intellectual capacity, for it to be dismissed out of hand as irrelevant or insignificant. What is more, it is an observable fact that not only among relatively primitive people or those who have not reached a high level of sophistication, but also among highly civilized groups who represent in themselves a developed scientific awareness, a religious attitude is frequently to be found. All this would appear to require careful attention to what men and women who take this attitude and who find it enormously important in their lives may have to tell us, or may have to show us, about the religious "adjustment," to use Henry Nelson Wieman's kind of language.

In this opening chapter I shall consider some matters that emerge in this context. First of these will be what might be styled the human attempt to get at or describe the ground of our feeling of worth. The second will have to do with the concept of the divine, of "God" to put it in traditional idiom, which can make sense in confirming this worth or value. Third, but in later chapters, we need to attend to the place which in one particular religious faith, namely Christianity, is given to the event toward which that faith is said to point and from which, indeed, it has taken its rise: the way in which the total reality of Jesus of Nazareth is believed to be what Bishop John Robinson has called "a window into God." Finally, and fourth, we must say something about the manner in which the convictions therein affirmed are communicated through a living tradition or witness that has persisted for some two thousand years and that even today exercises a very considerable influence and plays a very significant role in the experience of countless numbers of men and women. Obviously our discussion is at best "programmatic," as nowadays is said. Yet it may be suggestive and perhaps even helpful in any further consideration of the implications of the human sense of worth, from which we have started in our treatment of the subject.

I

I believe that we may say that all religious attitudes and adjustments include some affirmations about "ultimate explanation," some awareness of an object of reverence or worship, some feeling of moral requirement and moral empowering, and some sense of harmony or pattern.

Precisely because human beings are possessed of some degree of rationality and hence seek to explain whatever happens to them or whatever their experience seems to signify, they are impelled to look for a supreme and, so far as may be, all-inclusive explanation both of themselves and of the world in which they exist. It is natural for men and women to ask, "Why?"; and it is natural for them to attempt to go beyond or behind the immediately available answers to that persistent question—in other words, to look for what might be styled some "ultimate" meaning which both gives sense to, and makes sense of, experience in that world. Hence religions will produce "creeds," whether these happen to be formally stated or only implicitly accepted. If there is any worth or value, such as we seem always to assume (however often we neglect or even deny this fact), then it is logical to relate that sense or feeling to whatever may intellectually seem a meaningful way of speaking about such ultimate explanation. The various philosophies of religion, the differing metaphysical systems, provided they take with sufficient seriousness both this sense of worth and also the religious attitude so generally found, are ways in which an effort is made to provide a rational basis for this explanation.

Let us leave it at that, returning later to a treatment of one way, to me the most satisfactory way, of talking of this final explanation or meaning. We may proceed to observe that the religious attitude and adjustment, in its many different manifestations, seems also to include what I have called some awareness of a *that* which is taken to be a suitable, even a necessary, object of reverence or worship. Sometimes this does not show itself in formal acts but only in personal feelings of "worth-ship." It does not inevitably require some public occasion. In Islam, for instance, there are few if any "public services," although in most of the world's religions, both primitive and sophisticated, there are just such public activities. The exact *that* toward which reverence is felt, toward which worship is directed, is not our concern at the moment. All I am now interested in affirming is the widespread presence of this concern for expressing, in some fashion, just such reverence. Furthermore, I point out that however the *that* may be defined, it is directly associated with the "ultimate" explanation noted in the paragraph above. It would seem that genuine worship or reverence, in any demanding sense, can be given only to that for which a claim to "ultimacy" may be made. Any reverence for something less than this "ultimate" would be regarded as idolatrous. We may say, then, that "cult" is involved in religion.

Not only does the religious attitude and adjustment work itself out in terms of explanation and express itself through reverence or worship. It also carries with it a moral corollary: it speaks of a means for moral empowering which makes any proposed guidelines or rules a possibility for human living, however inadequate or deficient may be the outward manifestation of that possibility. If we can say that the general religious way includes a "creed" and a "cult," we can also say that it includes notions about "conduct." What these notions may be, how they may be proposed or stated, what requirements they may make upon those who participate in a given religious adjustment: these are secondary questions, although they are also matters of enormous importance for such participants. The *fact* is plain enough: not only is a "way of living" implicit in any religion about which we have information, but also some conviction is entertained about, and some experience is claimed of, a power or strength that is taken to be available for those who are sincerely prepared to accept the "creed" and engage in the "cult."

Finally, the concern which appears to be present in religious adjustment is more than a matter of explanation or right reverence or suitable conduct, with empowering to make this at least a meaningful possibility. The aim which comprehends within it these three factors is an aim towards harmony or patterning of human life. If the search for explanation is intellectual, the engagement in reverence emotional, and the presentation of moral demands conational, this aim at harmony may be called aesthetic—aesthetic, naturally, in the profound meaning suggested by the Greek word behind that English term, which has to do with "feeling-tones" and appreciative awareness leading to a kind of human living which is fulfilling and "abundant." The Hebrew word *shalom* is exactly what is in view here, for that word points toward much more than "peace" (which is its obvious meaning); it suggests a deep sense of "rightness" and carries with it something of the same significance as the *kalagathon* (beauty in goodness, goodness in beauty) about which Plato has Socrates speak at the conclusion of the *Phaedrus:* Plato tells how his great master, at the end of a night spent in discussion, went to the riverside and prayed, "O Pan, and whatever other gods dwell in this place, make me *kalagathos.*"

Rational or intellectual, emotional, conational or volitional, and aesthetic components are present, then, in the religious attitude, wherever known, however simple or complex, as this attitude is found in the various world religions and often enough too in apparently "secular" adjustments of human life which disclaim the *name* "religious" yet manifest the characteristics, functionally speaking, which more commonly are described by the use of that term.

II

We now turn to consider how best to indicate the nature of the divine reality taken to be in a profound sense the "ultimate" explanation or the ground for that sense of worth in human existence which I have urged is to be found in men and women— whether this is given definite statement or is felt only as a vague but inescapable *leit-motif* pervading our actual living experience in all its variety and with its varying degrees of intensity, whether keenly felt or dimly apprehended.

Alfred North Whitehead remarked that one of the unhappy aspects of much traditional thought about the divine reality has been its tendency to "pay God metaphysical compliments." By this he meant that all too often the divine has been defined as underived being-itself, as the single and all-sufficient entity, or as the only genuinely "real" reality, thus reducing the world of creation to the estate of a minor and relatively unimportant "avocation of the Absolute," to use another of his phrases. I wish to avoid this kind of approach; and in its place I shall suggest four qualities which may properly be said to provide as "ultimate" an explanation as we are likely or able to get. What can we say about a *that* for reverence which carries conviction and has an irresistible appeal; a moral "rightness" and a means for moral empowering that do not deny the genuine validity of creaturely existence and its importance and dignity; and a key to the harmonious or patterned life which religion takes to be its final aim insofar as human experience is concerned?

I suggest that we may tentatively define the divine reality as *(a)* unsurpassable by anything other than itself; *(b)* entirely worshipful; *(c)* utterly dependable and reliable, upon which everyone and everything rests, so that without it there would be anarchy or chaos in the world rather than cosmos and order; *(d)* the source of "refreshment and companionship" (to use, once again, a phrase of Whitehead's). I believe that we can arrive at some such definition—if that is the proper word here—by a consideration of the depths of human experience, on the one hand, and an observation of "how things go in the world we know," on the other. There is no possibility in this chapter for the further development of this last point; elsewhere I, and others too, have sought to present the case for it. At the moment, I must be content simply to affirm that what is here in view is a wide generalization from human experience, along with an insistence that whatever we say about the divine reality must not be said as if that reality were a complete anomaly, entirely different from such principles as are found necessary to make sense of that experience. Rather, it is to be understood as the "chief exemplification" (once more following Whitehead's thinking) of just those principles—always remembering that for us to say "*chief* exemplification" (notice my stressing the adjective in that phrase) is to point towards the "eminent" nature of the reality in question and not to reduce that reality to the status of *just another* instance of those principles. Simply put, God as the explanation, etc., is the supreme instantiation of exactly those categories which a careful analysis of experience, and of the world in which experience is had, requires if *any* explanation is to be reached at all. Thus we are delivered from foisting upon deity those qualities, attributes, or concepts which a long philosophical tradition (stemming from one element in Greek philosophical enquiry) has developed—and in so developing has

often made deity a metaphysical "monster," irrelevant and meaningless to men and women in their ordinary human experience.

For an explanation to be adequate, it must be such that no other
attempt at explaining can surpass it. It must be such that no matter what else may be the case, this unsurpassability must be accepted as final. But notice that the unsurpassable quality has reference only to *other* possibilities of explanation; it does not in any
way deny that the reality unsurpassable by *anything else* may not,
at a later moment, *surpass itself*. It may "enlarge" itself, become
more inclusive, and (if it should be a personalized reality, as for
religious adjustment, at least in the tradition we in the West inherit, it is taken to be) it may widen its "experience" so that in the
light of contributions from other realities it may have available
for it opportunities for further expression, precisely *as* being itself
unsurpassable. This entails something else, of course, to which at
a later point we shall return—namely, that the unsurpassable reality must also be in continuing relationship with those other and
surpassable realities which constitute what we call "the creation."

Once again, the unsurpassable reality is such that it may
properly be the object of reverence and worship. This kind of
attitude is appropriate *only* to that which is supreme; it cannot be
given to dependent or entirely contingent occasions or entities.
Nor can it be proper to worship that which is evil in itself. Worship, which (as we have noted earlier) signifies "worth-ship," is
proper only when it is directed towards that which *is,* so to say,
"worth-worthy"—that which in itself is good and by reason of its
goodness draws towards itself the grateful response of other and
surpassable entities. As the scholastic divines of the Middle Ages
correctly saw, only the *summum bonum* can be reverenced. The
distressing way in which humans may and do give worship to what
is evil does not contradict this point, since the evil is there worshipped as their good—*sub specie boni*, as the Scholastics insisted. There is a saying, "Evil, be thou my good"; but those who
say this are unconsciously, yet implicitly, affirming that there *is* a
worshipful good, even if that good is mistakenly or wickedly identified with what is truly evil in itself. The evil is *taken to be* good
by those who revere it. Hence, in spite of themselves, such persons
are in fact testifying that only the good *can* be adored.

Those who have a religious attitude also consider that the

divine reality, unsurpassable and good, is always dependable —it is unfailing in character, unceasing in concern, ever to be trusted.

This is the case even when circumstances may seem to argue otherwise: "Let him kill me if he will; I have no other hope than to justify my conduct in his eyes" (Job 13:15). In the last resort, we feel that this reality will not "let us down." In some sense or other, it can be counted on to abide faithful, just as in some sense its creative activity is the chief causative principle in the world. The testimony of the saints and seers is to the point here. However doubtful they may be in moments of despair or frustration or when they experience evil in any of its many forms, they tell us that ultimately they rely upon deity as upholding and maintaining them and the world, often in ways very mysterious and surprising.

Finally, the divine reality provides for human existence a refreshing experience, whether this is known in some vivid and compelling way or is only dimly hinted at by means of the common experience in which men and women, under great strain and with full recognition of their own frailty, find help. "Time the refreshing river" may be one such manifestation; so also may human companionship and assistance. But in the last resort, all these are taken by religious people to be nothing other than the working of the divine through creaturely agencies. Furthermore, the divine reality establishes some sense of a presence—again either vividly experienced or only vaguely felt—which indicates that "underneath are the everlasting arms"; which suggests that "the universe ultimately is friendly" however terrible it may seem on many occasions; and which convinces men and women that they are not, in the last resort, alone in a world which so often can seem to be careless or indifferent.

I should urge, therefore, that what might be styled "a working definition of God" includes as its ingredients just such factors: unsurpassability by anything other than itself, the capacity to evoke worship and reverence, the sense of an abiding durability which provides genuine dependability, and an awareness of some source of refreshment and companionship which enables men and women to find a grounding for their feeling that life has significance and value.

III

In the light of the considerations presented in the preceding sections, there are further statements which may be made, as part of a more specifically theological presentation of the supreme and divine reality, while at the same time avoiding unnecessary "metaphysical compliments."

First of all, the relationship between that reality and the created world must be seen as involving mutuality. The kind of absoluteness which removes the divine so far from the world and gives the divine such an independent and self-contained existence that the world is irrelevant is to be rejected as an instance of the pursuit of some supposed absolute substance, existing in and for and of itself, which makes talk about genuine unsurpassability, utter dependability, proper object of adoration, and source of refreshment and companionship tantamount to denying love as the central quality or attribute, the identifying characteristic, of deity.

For love *is* relationship. Furthermore, unrelatedness would also be a denial, not only of love in deity and as deity, but of the principle already enunciated: that the divine is *not* totally anomalous in respect to generalized principles of meaning but rather is their "chief exemplification." To put it in ordinary language, God must be influenced and affected by, as God also influences and affects, the world. God is in real and internal relationship with that world, not in a merely logical and external relationship.

But, secondly, if this be asserted, we must also assert that the world makes a difference to deity. From it God can and does receive; God's outgoing toward it is complemented by his openness to it. So the created order matters, not only to itself but also to the reality upon which it depends in some final sense. The picture of deity which denies that the divine reality is in some fashion genuinely dependent—for joy and in anguish—upon the world and what goes on there is a picture which is altogether too "complimentary," in a metaphysical sense. Religious attitudes do not require it; indeed, properly understood they negate that picture.

On the other hand, there is in the idea of divine "independence" one hint at truth. This intimation is found in the concern, in religious adjustment, that the supreme and divine reality shall be

deterministic

unchanging in basic character. In other words, it must be self-consistent in its nature. At this point we properly speak of the divine as unfailingly good, unfailingly just, unfailingly faithful to its purpose or aim. Yet to say this is also to suggest that in its relationships at different times and different places, the divine manner of operation or activity shall be adapted to the situations with which it has to deal. Thus we have both permanence, in respect to fundamental character, and possibility of change or alteration, in respect to the expression of that character.

For this to be true, there must be a sufficient "personeity" in deity to make such adaptation possible, as the divine is contemplated and relates itself to the creation. Thus deity is to be named a "he" and a "she"—with both masculine and feminine qualities, as we might put it—rather than an "it." Hence from now on I shall use these more personal pronouns, only regretting that in the English tongue we do not have a single pronoun which will be inclusive of masculine and feminine.

But how can God be known, not merely as a theological concept but also as a relational reality? The religious attitude commonly speaks of "faith" at this point. Some commitment must be given by the creature, some engagement of self accepted as a possibility, if such knowledge, relationally speaking, is to be available. It is here that we move toward an even more practical aspect of the religious position. Furthermore, it is highly important to recognize that when we talk about such personal awareness through commitment and engagement, we do not for a moment deny, nor do we in any sense minimize, what Whitehead called "the secular" aspect of the divine working. Religious attitude and adjustment can become intolerably narrow if lacking in a wider cosmic context and setting. In that case, God becomes merely a function of human religious thought and experience and is reduced to little more than the object of just such human existence. For deep religion, that will not do. Deep religious sensibility demands and implies the cosmic reference. "He has the *whole world* in his hands," says the song made familiar by its poignant rendering in the voice of Marian Anderson—and those words affirm, what here we necessarily assert, that human experience and human history have a *natural* setting. The existentialist dedication to the reality of human decision and its consequences is to be supplemented by the understanding that these are taking place *in the world* which is presented to us through observation of the order of nature. There are not two worlds but one. The two are neither separable nor isolable, although they may be distinguished. The so-called "world of religion" and the so-called "world of nature" are aspects of one single creation and therefore are not two worlds at all but simply and only *the one* world in its differing sorts of expression.

IV

In our opening discussion, I spoke of two other points which must have our attention. One was the place of Jesus of Nazareth as a "window into God"; the other was the living tradition which has conveyed through history the significance of that given event from which Christian faith takes its rise. Originally I had thought to consider these two points, at some length, in this opening chapter. But I have decided, on further thought, that I need only repeat them here and insist on their importance, and then (in later chapters) give them the detailed attention that they deserve. Especially in respect to the event of Christ, such detailed attention is demanded; I shall devote two whole chapters to it. I shall also look at the living tradition, doing this in a chapter whose concern will be the nature of tradition, its corollary in a conception of the ministering as functioning in and for tradition, and always with due regard for the way in which tradition secures its abiding significance if the religious attitude and adjustment called Christian is to continue to speak to succeeding generations of men and women.

2

Christian Theology after the "Death of God"

The furor of fifteen years ago over the "death of God" theology seems to have died down. William Hamilton, among the first who talked and wrote in this vein, has said lately that the "death of God" emphasis belongs to the past—the recent past, surely—and that today we must go beyond it. Whatever may have been the contribution it made, the contribution *has been* made. What has this movement to say to us today?

I do not myself subscribe to the view that theology works in the fashion which Hamilton's remark suggests—a sort of drunkard's progress, with no real direction and without obvious continuities. But I agree on three points: first, that the "death of God" literature *has* made a contribution to theology, even if it is not the contribution which its representatives might think; secondly, that the movement is just as dead as its leaders said that "God" was dead; and thirdly, that we must go forward to a doing of theology, in the Christian mode, which will take account of what that particular literature had to say. In this chapter I wish to speak of these three points.

The talk about the "death of God" was, I believe, an extraordinarily misleading, even if highly provocative, way of saying something important. What was really involved was the death of certain *concepts* of God, rather than a supposed death of God himself. One realizes that this interpretation was denied by Thomas Altizer and other advocates of the view; they insisted that they were talking about a genuine death of God as an historical occurrence. But even they show that the contrary is the case. Altizer himself demonstrated this when he claimed that he was talking about the absolute immanence or "presence-in-this-world" of the Word or Spirit, in consequence of the radical *kenosis* or self-emptying of the transcendent deity usually denoted by the word "God." That Word or Spirit most certainly is *not* dead; and Altizer's "gospel" was precisely the reality in human experience and in the world-order of the Word or Spirit with whom human beings must reckon whether they wish to do so or not.

I am convinced that what died, that whose death was stridently announced, is a series of models, images, pictures, or concepts of deity which for a very long time have been taken by considerable numbers of people to be the Christian way of understanding God. It is important in this connection to note that each of the three leading advocates of the position was in reaction against a notion of God that represents just such a series of models. Paul van Buren was a disciple of Karl Barth, under whom he wrote his excellent doctoral dissertation on Calvin's teaching about Christ as the true life of human beings. Hamilton was an opponent of natural theology in all its forms, even if he studied at St. Andrews under Donald Baillie; it was the so-called "neo-orthodox" line which had attracted him, theologically. Altizer was a slightly different case. He worked under Paul Tillich and with Mircea Eliade, but his reaction was *against* the aspects of Tillich's thought which stressed "being-itself" in God and *for* those aspects which emphasized the need for radical reconception of Christian thought.

Alfred North Whitehead wrote in *Process and Reality* many years ago that the Christian theological tradition has tended to conceive of God in three ways, each of them mistaken: as "the ruling Caesar, or the ruthless moralist, or the unmoved mover."[1] It has failed to give central place to what he styled "the Galilean vision," in which God is shown as persuasion or love. Hence, in his striking phrase, "the Church gave unto God the attributes which belonged exclusively to Caesar," seeing him "in the image of an imperial ruler," "in the image of a personification of moral energy," or "in the image of an ultimate philosophical principle." With certain qualifications I should say that Whitehead stated the facts here. In various combinations and with differing emphases, the concept of God with which many Christian thinkers have tended to work has been composed of exactly those ingredients: absolute power, stark moral demand, and unconditioned and essentially unrelated (in the sense of a two-way movement) "being-itself" as the ultimate cause of everything-not-God, but not in any way affected by that which was not itself—and the neuter here is highly significant, *ens realissimum*. Great theologians, like Augustine and Aquinas (to name but two), have written in this fashion; but they were also strangely discontented in doing so, since their "working" faith was in the biblical God of unfailing love-in-action, effecting his purpose of love in nature and history, and most profoundly open to and receptive of what went on in the world. Hence the ambiguity which (as I think) one can see running through so many of the great theologies.

But it was the stress on power, on "ruthless moralism," and on transcendence in the sense of nonrelationship, which many took to be demanded when one talked of God. Of course one might also add, almost as a kind of after-thought, "Oh yes, he is also loving." I do not parody here, for I myself have found that when I have tried to present a theological point of view which made the reality of love absolutely central, and put the other so-called divine attributes in a place secondary to that love, I have been met with the response, "Of course God is loving, but to talk of God we must begin with his omnipotence, his transcendence, his aseity (self-containedness and self-existence), his absolute righteousness with its consequent demands on human beings." This procedure seems to me to be entirely wrong, however traditional it may be. What we ought to do is to start with God self-disclosed in human affairs as love-in-action. Then, and only then, can we use (adverbially, as it were) the other so-called attributes. God as love-in-action is more than any particular expression of his love (hence he is transcendent); God as love-in-action is always available (hence he is immanent and omnipresent); God as love-in-action is able to envisage every situation in its deepest and truest reality and accommodate himself to it, so that he can indeed achieve his loving ends (hence he is omniscient); God as love-in-action is unswerving in his love, unfailing in its expression, unyielding in his desire to confront human beings with the just demands of love (hence God is righteous). If we had worked in that way, we should have been saved from some of our supposedly insoluble theological problems, many of which are based on taking the other, and as I think wrong, approach.

However this may be, the fact is that for very many contemporary men and women, not only of a sophisticated sort but also of quite ordinary attainments, the notion of God as absolute power, as unyielding moral dictator, and as metaphysical first cause never himself affected by the world, has gone dead. There are many reasons why this has happened. This chapter is no place to discuss them at length, but among others we may mention scientific understanding, psychological discoveries, awareness of sociological conditions, and all that Bonhoeffer summed up in saying that humankind has "come of age." By this he did *not* mean that the human being is an entirely mature and adult creature who now can take the place of God; he *did* mean that we now know our own responsibility and that God treats us, not like slaves nor like little children, but like sons and daughters to whom he entrusts such responsibility. This "going dead" of the notions I have mentioned was stated plainly for us in the writers who spoke of "the death of God."

So much for my first point. My second is to repeat that the movement called by that name is now itself a matter of the past; it has made its contribution, and that is that. It has taught us something, and by now we ought to have learned what it had to teach us. Of course the learning has not been done simultaneously in all parts of the Christian world or anywhere else. Hence for some of us, it might be said, the situation is still *pre*-"death of God"; and for those who are in this situation, the lesson is still to be learned. But for those who have got an inkling of what this is all about, who have learned the lesson, the situation is *post*-"death of God" and we must now go on to the constructive task.

I shall not spend time in showing how and why we are in that "post" era. I only call in witness the remark of Hamilton which I have already cited. He at least feels that the "calling in question," the denials, the stark affirmation of the "end of sheer transcendence, sheer moralism, sheer power" (as I like to put it), has been accomplished. So the problem for us, as for him, may be phrased in a typically American way: "Where do we go from here?" It is with that question that the remainder of this chapter will concern itself. But the one thing that is quite clear is that we cannot "go back," as if we could return to the older ideas and concepts quite unchanged by what has happened during the past few decades. If we cannot rest content in the denials, the "calling in question," and the like, neither can we retreat into the theologies of the past. This is what I find troublesome in the writing of E. L. Mascall on the subject. He has usually been sound in his criticisms of the "death of God" school and, indeed, of the whole "radical theology" which in one way or another is associated with it. But because of his failure to understand *why* such a theology in its various forms has appeared, he has been unable to see any other solution than a "return."

In going forward with Christian theology *after* "the death of God," we have several options. Let me mention some of them, assuming that we cannot work with Thomism (either "classical" or "revised"); nor with that peculiarly Anglican affair known as "liberal Catholicism," in the style of *Essays Catholic and Critical* [2] or the writings of Charles Gore; nor with "liberalism" in its reductionist form as found in Harnack or Harnack *redivivus;* nor with sheer biblicism in its fundamentalist dress. So I mention the following possibilities, some of them also mentioned in an excellent little book of lectures given in Chicago some year ago, *Philosophical Resources for Christian Thought,* [3] in which various conceptualities were discussed at length: (1) existentialism in some mode; (2) phenomenological (and in that sense nonmetaphysical) enquiry; (3) analytical philosophy and its talk about *bliks* and "language games"; (4) process thought in its several forms. To these four I should add the so-styled "secular theology" often advocated today, with a side-glance at revived and restated "biblical theology." Here are six possibilities.

Of some of them I must speak very briefly. For example, the kind of "biblical theology" sometimes advocated today assumes that we should go forward by taking with utmost seriousness the biblical images or motifs—not the literal, textual stuff of Scripture, which would involve us in a kind of new "fundamentalism," but the main-line series of biblical images. I am very much in sympathy with this approach, so far as it goes. For Christians the biblical images and patterns are of *first* importance, since it is from them that the Christian picture of God takes its rise. But it must be pointed out that these images and patterns are most diverse; further, they belong, in their explicit shape, to ages in which we do not ourselves live. Hence what is required is what Leonard Hodgson so often, and rightly, demanded: we must ask ourselves what the case *really is,* so far as we can grasp it today, if people who thought and wrote *like that* phrased it in the way they did. Otherwise we shall be using the Scriptures in a very wooden and unimaginative fashion, even if we do not succumb to literalism in its obvious sense. Furthermore, if we wish to communicate the deepest meaning of those images and patterns, we cannot rest content with them as they stand. That would be to resemble the Chinese who, when ship-wrecked on a desert island, made their living by taking in each others' laundry! We must translate if we wish to communicate.

In the second place, the use of analytical philosophy will help us enormously in the way in which we use words. It will enable us to clarify our language, to avoid contradiction, to stop talking sheer nonsense, to look for some kind of referent which will give the necessary verification to what we are saying as Christians. All this is of great importance, lest we fall into the temptation to use high-sounding words as an evasion of difficulties. It has been said that whenever some older theologians got to a hard place they simply quoted a few lines of Wordsworth or Tennyson, thinking that ended the matter; or that they made a few biblical citations as if that were the complete answer; or (at worst), that when the attack was most fierce, they used the word "mystery" as a kind of "escape-hatch." Analytical philosophy is a neutral discipline, for which we may be grateful. But it gives us no working conceptuality for the statement of the theological implications of Christian faith with the claims which that faith makes about "how things really go in the world."

Once more, in the third place, the kind of phenomenological method which is often suggested is of a non-metaphysical type. It is interested only in description, in terms of how living religion, as a matter of deepest intuitive observation, effectively operates in human experience in the world where human beings live. This is valuable; a Van der Leeuw, an Eliade, and others like them can help us a great deal. How does faith function, what embodiments does it have, what attitudes does it demand? These are questions which ought to be answered and I discussed them in the opening chapter. But I cannot think that their answer will provide the general conceptuality which we require if Christian faith is to be grounded in the stuff of reality and if the case for it is to be made in a manner which speaks meaningfully to the men and women for whom it exists and to whom it is supposed to address itself.

We are left then with three possibilities: "secular theology," existentialist theology, and process theology. I shall say something about each of them—and as my ordering indicates, I shall come down in favor of the last of the three as offering us the best conceptuality available today as we go forward from "the death of God."

The phrase "secular theology" may be taken to mean either one of two things: either a theology *of* the secular or a theology which *confines itself to* the secular realm. Since I have spoken critically of Dr. Mascall earlier in this chapter I am glad to say here that I believe that he has written admirably about this distinction in the last part of his *Theology and the Future*.[4] He has pointed out that a theology which is strictly *confined* to the world of "here and now" cannot take account of the ultimate questions which people must ask; whereas every sound Christian theology is indeed required to speak of that "here and now" and yet to relate it to God as creative principle and to see God at work in the immediacies of human existence in the whole range of what we style "secular existence." In other words, I agree that Christian faith must see God *in the world* but that it cannot remain content with "the world" as if it exhausted all there is of God. Whitehead once said that "God is in this world or he is nowhere"; that is entirely sound. But Whitehead also said that the world and God are not identical; and I should interpret this utterance, along with others by him, to mean that there is in the divine life an inexhaustibility or transcendence which makes possible the wonderful novelty which the created order manifests, disclosing what Gerard Manley Hopkins named "the dearest freshness deep down things."

In any event, if a "secular" approach to theology thinks that it avoids all metaphysical conceptions, it is profoundly mistaken. Of course one can mean what one wants by the word "metaphysical." If one intends to speak of a grandiose construction in terms of supernatural entities, with a schematic ordering of everything according to some superimposed pattern, metaphysics may well be denied. The present-day attack on metaphysics is probably nothing more than an attack on idealistic constructions of this type, after the fashion (say) of Hegel or Bradley. But metaphysics can also mean—and process thinkers would say that it ought to mean—the inevitable human enterprise of generalizations widely applied, on the basis of a particular point or event or experience taken as "important," to the rest of our experience of the world and the world which we surely experience. It can mean, then, the development of those principles which most adequately express what we experience and know, in the full range of our human encounters; and the result is a "vision" which can be tested by reference back to experience and to the world experienced. Metaphysics in this mode is not some highly speculative system imposed on the world. It is an induction from what is known of the world and also a demand that we act in the world, as Marx rightly insisted. Everybody engages in this, usually in a very naive manner; the philosopher is one who in a more sophisticated and critical manner engages in this attempt at making sense of things, including human experience.

The self-styled "secular theologian" is often doing exactly that. One has only to read Gregor Smith, whose untimely death we all lament, to observe this. Both in *The New Man*[5] and in *Secular Christianity*[6] Gregor Smith was actively setting forth *this* kind of metaphysics, taking as his "important" moment or event the historical encounters of men and women, specifically with Jesus, and from these developing a view of the generalized situation of "man-in-the-world" which, in my sense of the word, is inescapably metaphysical, even if he himself rejected the word and thought that he was also rejecting the enterprise. What he was rejecting, it turns out, was only that "supernaturalistic" species of metaphysics which idealistic philosophers set forth in a pretentious claim to encompass in their thought all things in earth and heaven. Thus "secular" theology in itself does nothing more than deny a particular kind of metaphysics and leaves open to us the possibility of interpreting the secular world, and everything else in human experience, in some other and more appropriate manner. So as I see it, the options which now remain are in fact two: either an existentialist approach or a process thought approach.

The existentialist approach in contemporary English-written

theology has been associated with two names: one is Paul Tillich, the other John Macquarrie. I cannot mention the name Tillich without reverence, for that great and good man was a dear friend of mine and I respected, honored, and loved him. His theology was an attempt to combine an existentialist analysis of the human situation with a Christian faith interpreted along the lines of German idealistic thought; he himself confessed that Schelling had been his great master. His method of a correlation of question and faith's answer to the question is, I believe, very suggestive and helpful; his masterly analysis of what it is like to be human is almost beyond criticism. But his final "system," as he used to call it, seems to me to be too abstract to convey the Christian gospel, although in his preaching he was anything but abstract. I think that Professor Macquarrie's efforts, especially in *Principles of Christian Theology,*[7] offer a much more "available" approach for most of us. His insistence that every existential analysis presupposes and includes ontological affirmations seems to me right and sound; his way of using Heideggerian thought is instructive. He takes the biblical images with utmost seriousness and employs them effectively as being determinative of the total picture of God-world-humankind in the light of Jesus Christ.

If I were to make any criticisms of this existentialist mode of theologizing it would be to say that it is not sufficiently regardful of nature, in the strict sense of the physical world and the material stuff of things. And I should add that it lacks something of the dynamism which I believe is required of any Christian theology, not only because of the dynamic quality of biblical thought itself but also (and more significantly) because of the evolutionary way of things which people like Teilhard de Chardin have so insistently pressed upon us. But I confess that *if* I did not find process theology more appealing I should opt for Macquarrie's approach. At the same time I must say that if those two criticisms of mine were met sufficiently, there would not be too much to differentiate his way from the one to which I now turn in conclusion.

It is not necessary for me to outline fully my reasons for preferring process thought. I have already indicated these in my book *Process Thought and the Christian Faith*[8] to which I may perhaps refer any who are interested; and I shall return to the subject in the next few chapters of the present book. It will suffice here if I note that process thought regards the world as a dynamic process of interrelated (and hence social) organisms or entities, whose intentional movement is toward shared good in widest and most inclusive expressions; and that it interprets deity along *those* lines. God is no unmoved mover, nor dictatorial Caesar, nor "ruthless moralist"; God is the cosmic Lover, both causative and affected, "first cause and final effect," as Schubert Ogden has so well phrased it. He is always *related,* hence always *relational;* he is eminently *temporal,* sharing in the ongoing which *is* time. His transcendence is in his sheer faithfulness to himself as love, in his inexhaustibility as lover, and in his capacity for endless adaption to circumstances in which his love may be active. He does not coerce; he lures and attracts and solicits and invites and then waits for free response from the creaturely agent, using such response (which he has incited by his providing "initial aims") to secure the decisions which enable the agent to make actual his own (the agent's) "subjective aim." In the historical realm and in human life he discloses himself, precisely as love-in-action, in the total event which we name Jesus Christ. Since his love-in-operation is his essential nature—he *is* love, which is his "root-attribute," not *aseity,* as the older theology claimed—the other things said about him (transcendence, immanence, omnipotence, omniscience, omnipresence, righteousness, etc.) are to be understood, as I have already urged, as adverbially descriptive of his *mode of being love,* rather than set up as separate or even as distinct attributions.

We live in a "becoming" world, not in a static machine-like world. And God himself is "on the move." Although he is never surpassed by anything in the creation, he can increase in the richness of his own experience and in the relationships which he has with that creation. He is the *living* God; in that sense, we may say (as the title of a book of mine dared to do) that God is "in process."[9] In other words, the basic point of the biblical images of God as the living, active, loving, righteous, personalizing agent is guaranteed.

But above all, since he is no dictator after the model of Caesar, no self-contained being after the model of the worst sort of person we know, no moralist after the model of the puritanical and negative code-maker, he is truly to be worshipped. Worship means "ascribing worth"; and this we can do only to a lovable because loving One. We cringe before power expressed coercively and arbitrarily; we tremble in the presence of rigid moralism, when we do not react against it in wild and desperate efforts to be ourselves; we can only be puzzled by the kind of absolute essence which is without effects from what goes on around and about it.

But we can worship, truly "ascribe worth," to the perfection or excellence which is love in its eminent and supreme form. God is that; hence he is adorable.

What is more, he is imitable. We are to imitate God. Both Aristotle and Plato said so, while Jesus gave it content by saying that we were to be "like our Father in heaven." When God is known as love-in-action, disclosed as that love by the event in which Jesus is central; when we are caught up into life "in love" (which, if 1 John 4 is right, *is* life "in God"), we are enabled to become what God intends us to be, created lovers who seek to do "the works of love." That is why we are here; that is our destiny—or else Christianity is a fraud.

3

"A Thing Is
What It Does":
A Discussion
of God's Nature

The title for this chapter is a dictum of Alfred North Whitehead's, found in *Adventures of Ideas* in the section where he is
discussing the relation of science and philosophy.[1] In the course of
this discussion he notes that in modern physics "a thing is what it
does" and goes on to say that "what it does" is to produce what he
styles a "stream of influence." I wish to use these remarks, by the
one who may rightly be called the founding father of process
thought, hence indirectly the father of process theology, as suggestive for our Christian thinking about God. Although Whitehead, in the immediate context, did not speak of God, the fact is
(as everyone who has read him will know) that in the words
quoted he would himself have found the wider generalization
which may be applied to any and every "actual entity," from God
to the "tiniest puff" of existence. We have his authority, therefore, for the kind of discussion with which we shall concern ourselves: in what sense *God* "is what [he] does," and in what sense
what he "does" effects a "stream of influence."

To speak in such terms is of course to deny immediately the
conventional notion that there are *things* which are discrete in
nature and which exist without necessary relationships. It is to

contradict the idea that there are "beings" or "substances" which may be simply located at a given time and place; and to contradict also the view that the universe is made up of an accumulation of such substances or beings, in varying patterns or arrangements. As we all know, modern physics has made this view impossible; while introspection into human experience ought to make it clear also that we do not know ourselves as instances of a general principle of substantial being, in our case supposedly derivative and imperfect. With the collapse of all that is signified by the phrase "Newtonian physics" and by later nineteenth-century developments—now useful only as an abstraction applicable to very limited fields—and with the appearance of the newer psychology with its insistence on the dynamic and energizing quality of the human experience of selfhood, we have moved to a quite different view of the world and of ourselves. Nowadays we talk of events, "energy-events" as John Hick has suggested, of movement and change, of what Whitehead himself styled "creative advance into novelty." If we use the word "thing" at all, as Whitehead does in our quotation, we do if for convenience' sake. We use it only as a kind of shorthand for a focusing or concretion at given points of a whole range of energies, drives, forces, and the like, which perish and give place to still another focus or concretion that builds upon and uses the earlier stage but also has its own novelty and freshness.

My own identity, too, is not in my being or possessing a "something" (call it soul or mind or what you will) to which are attached the various qualities which go to "make me up," and to which occasions "happen," leaving the enduring "something" unaffected. On the contrary, my identity is established by the fact that in a certain routing or path, from the *past* which I "inherit" and which provides the materials for my movement forward, in the *present relationships* in which I grasp and am grasped by occasions or events which have occurred in the environment (ultimately, this includes the whole cosmos), and with an aim toward *a future fulfillment* of potentialities by decisions which have cut off *this* and accepted *that* among relevant possibilities. All are bound together in a continuity of direction. I am *becoming* a man. That is my "subjective aim," and to effect it I use the past, live in the present, and move toward the future which (I trust) will be the fulfillment of "what I have it in me to become." When the word

"I" is used, as we do use it, it does not indicate a supra-successive substantial entity. It is a word that conveniently sums up this bringing-together of past, present, and intentional future or aim at a particular point. If I am "aware" of a "self," it is not awareness of any such supra-successive entity, but awareness of a routing or direction, a "way taken" or "to be taken" which is specifically my own.

Furthermore, both in the world and in myself I see that this "doing," which establishes an entity for what it is, has its consequences. Whitehead himself is said to have remarked to a student (Nels Ferré) that he would "characterize reality" in the following way: "It matters; and it has consequences." *It matters:* that is, it has value or importance; *it has consequences:* that is, its influence affects, for good or ill, the creative advance as it proceeds in the world.

Thus at every point we have a world of activity, not a world of immutable microcosmic or macrocosmic *things*. The aim throughout the process is for greater intensity and richer satisfaction of appetition or desire; and this suggests that a sound metaphysic will see that "the energetic activity considered in physics is the emotional intensity entertained in life."[2]

When we come to speak about God, understood as the perfect entity by whose agency possibility becomes actual, through provision of initial aim and through lure by mutual prehension throughout the cosmos, and as the recipient of the accomplishments of all occasions which have come to be, we may wonder if what has just been said can be applied to him. As the giver of the "refreshment and companionship at which religions aim,"[3] must he not be placed in an entirely different category? Those who think this would seem to be victims of the illusion that the only possible definition of "perfect" is unchangeableness, immutability, and impassibility. This was an idea familiar in much Greek philosophy; but it is certainly arbitrary. Cannot perfection mean endurance, faithfulness, stability of character, and steadfastness in aim? A person nourished by the Judeo-Christian and biblical type of thought should almost naturally believe this to be the case; although because of the enormous influence of a certain kind of Greek thought in the Christian tradition it is not always remembered. To this point we shall return.

At the moment it will suffice to quote the familiar words of

Whitehead in *Process and Reality* which we have already noted; "God is not to be treated as an exception to all metaphysical principles, invoked to save their collapse. He is their chief exemplification."[4] This saying must not be misunderstood. It does *not* mean that there are no distinctions or differences between God and other actual entities. For one thing, God endures and does not "perish." Furthermore, as Professor Sherburne has noted in his *Key to Whitehead's Process and Reality*[5], "the principles governing all actual entities are in some instances exemplified in a reverse way in God"—e.g., entities in the world of time-space originate with *physical prehensions* of occasions or data, but God in his "primordial nature" works with his *conceptual valuation* of "eternal objects." Again, while temporal entities move from physical to conceptual prehensions, God in his "consequent nature" (as affected by the world) receives by his physical prehensions those entities and their accomplishments. But the *general* principles hold true of both, despite this reversal. God is said by Whitehead to be "*chief* exemplification" (italics mine), not simply another instance of exemplification. Here Whitehead is asserting the "eminent" character (in the idiom of Scholastic philosophy the word *eminent* means: "in a supreme degree and with imperfections and defects absent") of the divine exemplification of the broad generalizations required to give sense to the world and ourselves as we know these to be.

With this caution, we can observe that the point of the famous sentence in *Process and Reality* is to avoid a view of God which would equate the concept of God with the notion that he is simply "the unmoved mover" and hence would combine this with other ideas to produce a picture of deity as removed from relationship with creation, as self-contained in his existence, and as untouched by what happens in the world. He then becomes, as I have already remarked, to all intents and purposes "the ruling Caesar, or the ruthless moralist, or the unmoved mover," in which a supposedly immutable divine reality is interpreted after the model of an imperial despot or an arbitrary law-giver whose fiat must be obeyed by his creatures without question, at the risk of punishment or eternal damnation. All such views Whitehead regarded as idols; and he noted that they have slight contact, if any, with "the brief Galilean vision of humility" which "dwells upon the tender elements in the world, which slowly and in quietness operate by love."⁶ Whitehead's concept of God is integrally related to his total view of the world. God is neither an addendum to that view nor a logical contruct reached by "degrees of abstraction" (in Jacques Maritain's phrase) in an effort to arrive at some entirely nontemporal and supracosmic "first cause." In process theology, as I said earlier, the divine metaphysical attributes can only be understood and used *adverbially*.

Hence with God, as with everything else, we may say that "he is what he does" and that what he does is to produce a stream of influence which has its consequences in the creation, while it also has its effect on God's own "consequent nature" as he accepts or receives from the word; and as he finds increased intensity of selfhood in employing what he has received for further activity in the world of temporal actual entities.

What, then, does God *do?* And what are the consequences of that doing, the "stream of influence" which results from his activity?

In attempting to provide an answer to these questions, we shall now speak from the specifically Christian position—which, incidentally, at this point would not be called in question by Whitehead himself, although here our purpose is not to paraphrase his views but to work toward a Christian theological understanding of the divine nature and action in the world. Nonetheless Whitehead has given us the clue when he writes about the "Galilean vision" where *love* is revealed as "the nature of God and . . . his agency in the world"; and he adds the comment, "Can there be any doubt that the power of Christianity lies in its revelation in act, of that which Plato divined in theory?"—namely, "that the divine element in the world is to be conceived as a persuasive agency and not as a coercive agency."⁷

The short answer to the two questions posed above may thus be given: What God *does* is act always in love. Hence he *is* Love or Lover. And the "stream of influence" which is the consequence of his acting in love is the growth of the creation toward, and in, relationships characterized by love. But this short answer must be spelled out at greater length.

First of all, to say that God's "doings" are acts in love is not to say that he is weak, spineless, sentimental, or careless about results. Indeed the very fact that he is the chief causative agency in the world, working through provision of initial aim, through lure, and through capacity to receive into himself the creation's achievements, requires us to see that his loving activity is strong and effectual. God works justly and toward justice. He works according to his purpose or aim; he sets the limits within which the creative advance into novelty may proceed. He uses a minimal measure of coercion in the lower ranges of creaturely existence where this may be required (although this is always with loving purpose). And he "negatively prehends," or rejects from his "consequent nature," the surd of evil or wrong in the world. At the same time, however, his wisdom is able to extract from such evil or wrong whatever elements of good may be hidden there; and he can make "even the wrath of man" serve as an occasion for realization of a good which otherwise might not be possible. Hence his loving activity is more like that of an eminently good person who with great insight and foresight can see probable consequences, than it is like that of a weak person who is imposed upon by everyone and seems to have no mind or purpose of his own. Perhaps we may best say all this by citing the fine lines of an ancient Christian hymn, which speaks of God as "the strength of all creation"—the ultimate dependability, self-consistent and entirely trustworthy in his exercise of love. This is what omnipotence must mean, just as omniscience means the wisdom of love and omnipresence love's universal availability.

In further detail, what God does may be stated under several headings, to some of which we have already alluded. He provides for each occasion in the cosmos its "initial aim" in accordance with his over-all purpose of the achievement of the highest intensity of experience—which at the human level is justice and freedom towards growingly intimate relationships in love. From the continuum of possibility, this or that *special* aim is selected. It is then supplied to the concrescent entity, but not as an addendum; the entity emerges as and with this aim. What God is doing here is so grading or estimating relevance that he can act and does act with a specific end in view—his "particular providence for particular occasions," as Whitehead styles it.[8] And this is "the love of God for the world," since here we have a utilization of earlier achievements in creation which have been received by God in his "consequent nature" and now "pass back into the temporal world." For the "initial aim" is not an abstraction from the realm of possibility but in its effective working is qualified by earlier occurrences in the unending creative advance.

God also acts in employing for his purposes the proximate occasions by which each entity is grasped and which in its turn it grasps by its own decisions. Those occasions have their own integrity and the decisions which are made are made by the creature itself. Yet insofar as in their concrete actuality they are instrumental for the divine purpose of realized good, they are (as it were) the surrogates through which God works to lure towards the right choices for genuine fulfillment of possibility. In other words, his way of "doing" is not so much a matter of pushing, shoving, forcing, or externally controlling, as it is one of eliciting the entity's response which it gives because it senses that such a response is for its own best growth.

In setting the limits of creative advance, God also provides the necessary controls so that wrong decisions, or those which are mutually contradictory, do not get utterly out of hand. Evil and wrong are real enough; but they cannot over-pass those limits. Here once again the divine justice is manifested. Contrast is good, making possible richer aesthetic harmony. But is must not go to the point of a conflict which might ruin the whole enterprise; or when it does approach this, some means must be found to resolve the conflict by provision of a goal which will satisfy what is legitimate in each party to the conflict. Thus God acts as the "peacemaker" in creation.

He also acts to welcome into his own experience the goods achieved. To this we have referred earlier. Here it is important to notice that in thus receiving the achieved good, which can then "flood back" into the world in further movement of advance, God's love cannot fail to treasure whatever is valuable yet never will give its blessing to evil as such. So he judges in wisdom and comprehension and with tenderness, using what "in the temporal world is mere wreckage."[9] This is "a tender care that nothing be lost"; but this statement is at once to be qualified by saying that it "loses nothing *that can be saved*."[10] Our point here is that among the activities of God, one of his "doings" is "judgment on the world," but always judgment in love. Unlike the representation

of judgment in some theologies, however, we have here no arbitrary approval or dismissal, but rather a concern for the world in
"its sufferings, its sorrows, its failures, its triumphs, its immediacies of joy—woven by rightness of feeling into the harmony of
the universal feeling which is always immediate, always many,
always one, always with novel advance, moving onward, and
never perishing."[11]

This is something of what God "does"; and since "he is what he
does," we conclude that he is cosmic Lover. Our best image for
God, then, is a cosmic Love which is ceaselessly active. This is
very different from the picture of a static God condescending to
the world, although what such ideas have perhaps unconsciously
sought to assert is retained. What they have been striving to assert, with the use of concepts that sadly are ultimately destructive
of the insistence on God's "nature and his name as Love," is that
he endures, not beyond all "change and chance" but in and
through and with the employment of that change and chance
which is the condition of a world marked by boundless creativity,
with an enormous variety of focusing and of concrete instances.

We may now turn again to the "stream of influence" which is
the consequence of what God does. We have hinted at this in what
has already been said; but let us now put it in Whitehead's own
words: "What is done in the world is transformed into a reality in
heaven, and the reality in heaven passes back into the world. By
reason of this reciprocal relation, the love in the world passes into
the love in heaven, and floods back again into the world."[12] And
Whitehead then comments, "In this sense, God is the great companion—the fellow-sufferer who understands." The "stream of
influence" is God's loving use of the intensities reached in the
creation here and there, by this and that occasion. As each
achieves its satisfaction or fulfillment and *as such* "perishes," it is
not lost forever. It is not "cast as rubbish to the void." Taken by
God into his own experience, it is now available for him to use as
he provides new aims for new occasions. His influence is thus
effective for the realization of further good, in other ways and
other instances. As we have seen, this is always with a "tenderness" which lovingly uses what is there for God to use. But once
again, there is no substitution of coercion for persuasion; the introduction of new lures invites a free response in the affirma-

tive—yet there is no coercing of any agent to accept. There is always the possibility and tragically (as we know) the sheer fact of a negative response, where the divine lure meets refusal. Then the wisdom of God seeks for other ways in which his influence may be exerted towards the attainment of his goal.

The *ultimate* consequence is perhaps most suitably described by a word used by Teilhard de Chardin: *amorization*. Whitehead and Teilhard each developed his worldview independently, yet there are many remarkable similarities between them; here is an instance. Amorization means the development in creation of a relationship in which all creaturely constituents are caught up into and share in a love which is fulfilling for each and fulfilling for all. God's influence, streaming into the world at every point, is concerned for the growing realization of just that relationship. At each level, naturally, it will be manifested in the appropriate manner. At the *human* level, it will be a society of men and women in and under God, where love is "sole sovereign lord" and where everything thought, said, or done will be in love, by love, and for love. Here is mutuality at its highest possible level. Here is the realization of a just society. Indeed, it is the kingdom or reign of God.

This reign of God's love is not static, however. It includes within its harmony what goes on in the world; but it actively returns to the world to continue its invitation to succeeding occasions, luring them to share too in its beauty. We need not discuss here whether or not this requires that there be some continuing conscious awareness (in a finite and temporal sense of the term) on the part of those living entities which thus could "know," subjectively, what is taking place. Whitehead himself leaves the question open. But we can at least say that "nothing" which is truly good is "lost" in that reign where love is supreme.

It is my conviction that along some such lines as I have sketched we can work toward a doctrine of God which will be true to the "Galilean vision" and true also to the experience of men and women. But what is more, this way of understanding the divine nature is not primarily a matter of philosophical speculation; nor does it remain theoretical. It demands action to change the world. It is based upon and developed from that "revelation in act" (as Whitehead put it, referring to the impact of what he would have styled the *important* occasion, Jesus Christ), which sums up and both crowns and corrects everything else in biblical—and more general—disclosure of "how things go" in the world. It is Christocentric but not "Jesuolatrous." Jesus is not the supreme anomaly or "freak," but the classical (and hence supremely consequential or "result-full") instance. It requires a christological grounding, although it is not *confined* to that instance. As I should put it, God's "doing" is *defined* but not confined in the event we name Jesus Christ.

4

Reconception and Renewal of Christian Faith

The subject of this chapter is the further reconception or re-thinking of Christian faith with its result in a renewal of the impact of that faith, approached from perspectives and suggestions found (as we have seen) in the writings of Alfred North Whitehead, the Anglo-American philosopher whose general "vision of reality" is for some of us the best available insight into how things are and go in the world. In order to give this use of Whitehead a focus, the book which in this chapter will be our principal resource is *Religion in the Making,*[1] the Lowell Lectures delivered by him in King's Chapel, Boston, in 1926.

I begin however with some other quotations and comments of Whitehead, recalling that in *Adventures of Ideas* he had spoken of the need for what he styled a "new reformation" which would stress the central affirmation of Christianity, that God is to be seen as a persuasive rather than coercive force, derived from the "Galilean vision" in which Jesus is taken as disclosing both the nature of God and his activity in the world, and also of the need for the endeavor to express this in such a way that modern men and women would find it speaking directly to their need for what he had called "refreshment and companionship" in their experience.[2]

In his Lowell Lectures, Whitehead contrasted Buddhism and Christianity, the two great world religions, in this manner: "Buddhism and Christianity find their origins respectively in two in-spired moments of history: the life of the Buddha, and the life of Christ. The Buddha gave his doctrine to enlighten the world: Christ gave his life. It is for Christians to discern the doctrine." He then went on to say, "We do not possess a systematic detailed record of the life of Christ; but we do possess a peculiarly vivid record of the first response to it in the minds of the first group of the disciples after the lapse of some years, with their recollections, interpretations, and incipient formulations."[3]

The fact of the life of Christ, known through the response made to it, is therefore the center of Christianity. That life "is not an exhibition of over-ruling power. Its glory is for those who discern it, and not for the world. Its power lies in its absence of force. It has the decisiveness of a supreme ideal, and that is why the history of the world divides at this point of time."[4] Later Christian faith is, so to say, a response made to the initial response. This is shown in what he calls "responsive expression, namely expression which expresses intuitions elicited by the expression of others"; in this way "what is permanent, important, and widely spread, receives more and more a clear definition."[5] Thus we can say that ac-quaintance with the record of the primary response of the disci-ples in the primitive Christian community awakens in succeeding years, even in our own day, a response which in its turn provides them with the insight of faith. This insight is to be understood as establishing an "appeal to the direct intuition of special occasions"—in this case the "special occasion" of the life, teach-ing, and achievement of Jesus Christ, as a concrete occurrence in history—with the assurance that this "direct intuition" is "yet of universal validity, to be applied by faith to the ordering of all experience."[6]

Whitehead believed that a formulation of the originating in-sight, in terms of the response made to it, must take place if there is to be any genuine communication of its value to other persons and later ages. This is how "the element of novelty" in the pri-mary fact continues "forever [to evoke] its proper response." But such a formulation, which elsewhere he calls a "dogma," ex-presses something beyond itself. "The formula . . . is secondary to its meaning; it is, in a sense, a literary device. The formula sinks in importance, or even is abandoned, but its meaning remains

fructifying in the world, finding new expression to suit new circumstances. The formula was not wrong, but it was limited to its
own sphere of thought."[7] Any and every verbal statement of faith,
made into a formulation which can be communicated from one
person to another, is inevitably expressed in terms of the patterns
of thought, with the general assumptions and the attitude toward
the world, which prevailed at the time of that formulation's statement. If we assume that the literal and exact terminology of the
statement is absolutely final, then we must also assume that there
is "a commensurate finality for the sphere of thought within
which it arose. If the dogmas of the Christian Church from the
second to the sixth centuries express finally and sufficiently the
truths concerning the topics about which they deal, then the
Greek philosophy of the period had developed a system of ideas
of equal finality."[8] Obviously we can make no such assertion. We
do *not* think that Greek philosophy of the Hellenistic age had any
such finality. Thus "a dogma—in the sense of a precise
statement—can never be final; it can only be adequate."[9]

The task which faces succeeding ages is some kind of reconception of the "meaning" of the formulation. But does this not open
the door to alterations which may entirely destroy genuine identity? Whitehead handled this question as follows: "The great in-
stantaneous conviction . . . becomes the Gospel, the good news.
It insists on its universality, because it is either that or a passing
fancy. The conversion of the Gentiles is both the effect of truth
and the test of truth. Thus simplicity of inspiration has passed
from its first expression into responsive experience. It then dis-
engages itself from particular experience by formulation in precise dogmas, and so faces the transformation of history. In this
passage a religion coalesces with other factors in human life. It is
expanded, explained, modified, adapted. If it was originally
founded upon truth, *it maintains its identity by its recurrence to
the inspired simplicity of its origin.*"[10] That is to say, the identity in
continuity of the Christian tradition is secured by a constant appeal to its "formative" age, which then becomes for us "normative," to use my own words here. But normative is not meant in
the sense of requiring us to imitate, like copy-cats, the exact
phrasing in which that original event was described by those
closest to it; but rather by providing us with the "intuition," as

Whitehead would say, which was there expressed in an idiom appropriate to the time when it was put down in writing.

Finally, Whitehead's frequent stress on solitariness, so often entirely misunderstood, does not suggest that for him vital religion is confined to the inner moments when one is isolated from his or her fellows in a deep experience of confrontation with "what is permanent in the nature of things."[11] Indeed he explicitly states that "there is no such thing as absolute solitariness. Each entity requires its environment. Thus man cannot seclude himself from society."[12] This suggests that the Christian community is the place where the religious meeting with God takes place and hence the place where reconception and renewal must also take place. At the same time, such a social setting and context must not deny the utter centrality of each believer's own "worth of character" and his "internal life" as a person of faith, where "the force of belief [is in] cleansing the inward parts."[13] We might paraphrase this by saying that the reconception of faith, if it is to be valid, must have its renewing effect on the believer and lead to appropriate action in the world. It is no affair simply of the institution in its organized form, although it includes this; but essentially it is concerned with making it possible for each person to be utterly honest or sincere in what he or she believes and what he or she does—"the primary religious virtue is sincerity, a penetrating sincerity."[14]

So much for Whitehead's position. It must be said in passing that the more one ponders his words and grasps his thought, in this particular sphere as well as in other areas, one is increasingly astounded by his extraordinary penetration and insight. Despite the occasional very real difficulty of his language, what he has to say is so patently true to the deepest experience of men and women and the inner heart of living religion, that every time one returns to his writings one is rewarded with new insight and more profound understanding of what religious faith really means and how it can be maintained and purified. But let us now attempt to use this material from Whitehead as the basis for our own consideration of reconception and renewal.

That we face this task today, as perhaps never before in Christian history, must be obvious to any thinking Christian. We need only sketch here the various reasons which make the task so imperative—the advance of science and the wide dissemination of its method, approach, and conclusions; the increasingly obvious secularization of our culture; knowledge of religious traditions other than Christian, with the obvious appeal they have not only to their own adherents but to many brought up in a Western and supposedly Christian outlook; critical study of the Bible and particularly of the New Testament, sometimes with disconcerting results; the rise of avowedly atheistic states in Europe and Asia, along with the practical atheism of so many other nations; the moral collapse which has followed the breakdown of the older Puritanical biblical ethic and the Catholic ethic of natural law; the growing number of people who feel that the religious attitude is meaningless or "world-denying"; the startling depersonalization which makes "solitariness," as a person confronts reality and tries to come to terms with it, more and more difficult to attain. Nor can we forget the increasing demands for social justice, which "organized religion" has so often seemed to neglect. These are some of the factors which have so altered the position of the Christian community in the world, and so called into question the validity of its inherited formulations of belief and moral principles, that radical thinking, radical revision, and radical alteration of Christian stance and action are required. Without this there would seem to be little possibility of the Christian faith, which some of us hold very dear and which we believe to be true, continuing to mean much to anybody save to the small band who just happen to "like that sort of thing."

Now in this situation, we can be much helped (I am convinced) by making use of Whitehead's thought as summarized in our preceding pages. I believe that there are four points to which we may well give our attention as we undertake this imperative task of reconception, in the hope of eventual renewal. I list them first; then I shall speak of each. They are:

1. Christian faith had its origin in, and constantly refers back to, *a fact*—an event in history, whose center is Jesus Christ, understood as disclosing "the divine nature and agency in the world." The Christian community conveys this fact to us today.

2. This fact, if it is to be made significant, requires interpretation of its meaning and action to make it come alive in practice. It cannot be left to momentary expressions of feelings nor exempted

from the claim to intellectual respectability and practical expression in working for a world where the fact becomes manifest in deed. Both are congruous with the given *datum* and also coherent with the general picture we entertain of the world and human experience.

3. The formulations of that interpretation, which we have inherited from our long theological tradition, are not absolute or final. They had a meaning which they conveyed in an idiom suitable for the ages in which they were developed. What is required today is a deep empathetic grasp of that enduring meaning, with an equally earnest attempt to express it in an idiom suited for our own time.

4. Among the possible conceptualities available to us for this purpose, I argue that the Whiteheadian process philosophy is best suited for such reconception, if it is taken not as some entirely conclusive and final account of things but as a vision which provides a wide and inclusive way of seeing how the world goes, why it goes, where it is going, and what it requires of its adherents.

We shall consider each of these points in turn. But before doing so, I should like to recall, in this connection, a fruitful suggestion of John Robinson, whose first effort at reconception (in his best-selling *Honest to God*)[15] caused such a furor a few years ago. In a later book, *The New Reformation*[16] (did he get that title from Whitehead or some other source, one wonders?), Robinson notes that there are three kinds of approach to this problem of Christianity in the contemporary world. There is the *reactionary* one, which rejects all thought of reconception and is content to remain with the old formulations, because they have served well and are hallowed by long centuries of acceptance and use. Robinson believes, rightly I am sure, that this attitude is impossible today for any really thoughtful Christian, above all for any serious Christian thinker. The second approach he calls *revolutionary*. The man or woman who takes that approach is impatient with the inherited formulations (and with almost everything else in the Christian tradition, too). Such a person sees that they may have had some value in the past, but is sure that they have none in our time. Hence he or she would jettison them, sweep them away from the scene, and start from scratch, thinking that what is needed is an entirely new beginning, with no regard for what our ancestors in the faith have left us. In fact, a person like that "reeks of contemporaneity," as a naughty acquaintance of mine once put it. Robinson is convinced that this negative or destructive attitude is as impossible as the reactionary one; the latter would keep things exactly as they have been, while the former would dismiss the past in an uncritical and naive way.

The third possible approach is the *radical* one. Robinson points out that this word derives from the Latin *radix* (root); and he remarks that although it has often been used as a synonym for "revolutionary" it is really quite different in meaning. The radical wants to get at the roots of the tradition which one has inherited and in which one stands, and to discover through what I have styled "empathetic awareness" the deep intention of past formulations and practices. There is in them something of enormous value and importance which must be grasped; then, having been grasped, this must be stated once again in a manner that will communicate it to one's contemporaries. Unlike the reactionary, the radical is unable to remain in the past; unlike the revolutionary, the radical refuses to jettison the rich inheritance which is ours. The radical's urgent desire is to reconceive that inheritance and hence renew its attraction because it can now be seen as genuinely in contact with the truth about God, humankind, and the world.

I believe that Robinson's commendation of this last approach or attitude is right; and I hope that in what follows I shall be seen as neither reactionary nor revolutionary but radical. For I value the great Christian tradition; I regard it as a precious heritage; I cannot contemplate a light rejection of it. At the same time I see its serious deficiencies for our day; I believe it has little to say, *as it stands*, to my contemporaries; and I urgently desire what White-head called "expansion, explanation, modification, and adaptation" of the tradition and its ancient formulations, modes of worship and prayer, and principles of moral thought and practice.

1. Our first point, it will be recalled, was that Christian faith had its origins in, and constantly refers back to, a fact—an event in history, whose center is Jesus Christ. I cannot fail here to give myself—and I hope others—the pleasure of quoting Whitehead's strikingly beautiful words from *Adventures of Ideas* in which he wrote about "the supreme moment in religious history, according to the Christian religion."[17] He went on to say, "The essence of

Christianity is the appeal to the life of Christ as a revelation of the nature of God and of his agency in the world. The record is fragmentary, inconsistent, and uncertain. It is not necessary for me to express any opinion as to the proper reconstruction of the most likely tale of historic fact. . . . But there can be no doubt as to what elements in the record have evoked a response from all that is best in human nature. The Mother, the Child, and the bare manger: the lowly man, homeless and self-forgetful, with his message of peace, love, and sympathy: the suffering, the agony, the tender words as life ebbed, the final despair: and the whole with the authority of supreme victory." On this Whitehead commented, "Can there be any doubt that the power of Christianity lies in its revelation in act, of that which Plato divined in theory?"—and what Plato divined and Christ enacted was that "the divine element in the world is to be conceived as a persuasive agency and not as a coercive agency." From this fact we see that "God is love," as the Johannine writer puts it, since "the love I speak of is not our love for God, but the love he showed to us in sending his Son" (1 John 4:10).

In our day it is hardly necessary to emphasize this priority of the historical fact. In most Christian circles it is not only recognized but assumed as a given truth that prior to all formulations there is God's action of self-revelation in human affairs, a self-disclosure that is made in many different ways but chiefly in events in which God is believed to have been signally active. Perhaps William Temple's discussion in *Nature, Man, and God*[18] has been most influential in English-speaking lands in making this necessity clear. In their various ways the so-called "neo-orthodox" theologians made the same point, although with a narrower interpretation of revelation. But Temple is of particular interest to us here for still another reason. He urged that the *objective act* in history awakens the *subjective response* of believers; and that it is in what he styled the "coincidence of divinely-guided event and divinely-inspired response" that revelation is found. If we had only the former it could not *reveal* since there would be nobody at "the receiving end"; while if we had only the latter, the believer would be in danger of lapsing into subjective fancies and projections of his or her own notions about the universe. It is plain that here Temple, consciously or not, spoke in much the same vein as Whitehead in the passages we have already cited.

One futher comment may be made, however. The concept of "importance" in Whitehead's thought can be of assistance to us in making sense of the speciality of the event of Christ in the whole continuing series of contacts between God and humanity. For Whitehead, as he developed this concept, especially in his book *Modes of Thought*, an event has "value" or is "important" when it is sufficiently vivid or striking to awaken attention and interest in those who see or know it. It is also "important" when it illuminates the *past* which has made it possible at a given time or place, throws light on the *contemporary* situation, and provides a direction for the *future*. As it thus makes its impact on the observer, it evokes response, in which that observer recognizes and accepts what is disclosed as significant for him or for her. It *makes* sense to one and it *gives* sense to one's experience. This concept can be helpfully employed in respect to our Christian claim that in some way or other, in the constellation of occasions in which Jesus is the central and unifying figure, there is a novel disclosure which is yet in continuity with the past and indicative of the future. But I must not try to develop this theme now; it will be urged in a later chapter in this book.

In our effort at reconception, then, we must start from the *fact*, from the given reality of the event of Christ. And to that fact we must return, in order to maintain what (as we have seen) Whitehead styled "identity." As he said, this is to be done by "recurrence to the inspired simplicity" of a religion's origins. For us this means the New Testament record, with the Old Testament studied to learn how the newer revelation came to be. Naturally this will be no wooden appeal to the letter of the scriptural material, but a grasping of its main emphases and a deepening awareness of what those emphases were by way of asserting. We wish to reconceive the *Christian* message, not simply the general religious outlook; this desire is integral to our commitment and we dare not barter away our own distinctive heritage. Nor do our contemporaries want us to do this, for many indications show that the figure of Jesus (very often misunderstood or misinterpreted, alas!) still makes its perennial appeal. People believe that in some way or other he is indeed "important," although they may not quite know what to make of the One whom young people have recently named "Jesus Christ Super-Star."

2. Our second point was that the given event or fact requires

interpretation of its meaning, if it is to be communicated. This entails affirmations which are inescapable for us in our efforts to show the significance of the fact.

As Whitehead saw, the first centuries of Christian history were largely devoted to this enterprise. The dreary story of christological controversy, with its trinitarian supplement, is not to be dismissed out of hand. Harnack and other liberals of an older day may have spoken of the contamination of the simple evangelical word by the influence of Hellenism; they may have thought that the gospel had been so altered that it was no longer the one preached by Jesus himself. But they failed to see that the whole point of Christianity is that he who first proclaimed the good news of the coming Kingdom was inevitably made into the one who was himself to be proclaimed—and this for the reason that from the very earliest times, even during his days in Palestine, Jesus evoked the kind of response which made *him* as important as the message he proclaimed. The process continues in the Pauline literature and reaches its New Testament peak in John and in Hebrews. From there it was carried on by the theologians of the Church, who (granted all their faults) were intent on relating the overwhelming reality of new life in Christ Jesus to the whole of history, the cosmic situation, and God himself. The creedal formulations, and the definition of Chalcedon A.D. 451, cannot rightly be taken as nothing save examples of speculative argument or logical hair-splitting. They were attempts to do just what Whitehead saw must be necessary: the statement in some form of words of the significance of the originating event. This is the way the faith could "face the transformation of history" without loss of its essential self-identity.

I wish on this point to make but one remark. I am sure that in our necessary job of reconception we must attend respectfully to the labors of our ancestors in the Christian community and especially to the meaning which they sought to state in their formulations. Their language is not ours, their philosophical presuppositions are outmoded, and their too-precise language is a wrong attempt to capture in human idiom the mystery of the event—a mystery which attaches to any and every event but *a fortiori* to this one. I make this point about respectful attention to the old creedal and doctrinal statements because I am frequently appalled by the ease with which some Christian thinkers simply dismiss them, often in an almost contemptuous fashion. To adopt this attitude is to fail in historical imagination; it is also to make the stupid assumption that anything anybody thought before our own age is not worth considering. Our fathers in the faith were not infallible but they were not fools either. We should listen to what they have to tell us, even while we try to discover for ourselves a better way of doing in our day the job which they sought to do in theirs.

3. We have already anticipated the third point. The formulations which we have inherited are neither absolute nor final; yet the meaning they suggest is essential to the Christian reality. Our task in reconception is to find and employ other words to say the same thing.

But in putting it that way I have misstated the situation. When Vincent of Lerins in the ancient Church wrote *non nova sed nove*, "not new things but in a new way," his intention is plain; but he put it too simply. The truth is that when we state things "in a new way," we are also stating "new things," for the reason which Whitehead indicated when he wrote of the obvious way in which the dogmas of the second to sixth centuries were impregnated by the Greek philosophy of the time. The very things they stated were seen in the context of that type of thought; they cannot be lifted out of their context, translated exactly into another language, and then be thought to convey to us in our time exactly what they conveyed to them in theirs. "Context alters content," it has been said; and we must always bear this in mind.

Let me give an example. Most Christians would agree that in some fashion or other Jesus Christ is both "special" and (to use a rather dangerous word in this context) "transcendent" to other instances of God's self-revelation or expressive activity. Ancient Christian theology could state this only by using available concepts. Hence there was an inevitable placing of Jesus in a position almost *absolutely* unique; he was *so* special and *so* transcendent that he was taken to be without genuine relationship with other men and women or with God's more general movement in the world—although here an honorable exception must be made of the Alexandrine Fathers and some of the early Apologists. As later centuries followed the line which this earlier theological approach had laid down, Jesus was increasingly seen as an intrusion *abextra* into the world. In our own time one Christian thinker has even spoken of "the Incarnation as a divine rescue-expedition," as if God were absent from his world apart from Jesus and then came into it in a sudden and entirely unparalleled fashion.

Now I propose that for us today there must be other and more suitable ways of maintaining this speciality and (if you will) transcendence. I have suggested that Whitehead's concept of "importance" can help us here. But whatever device we employ, we ought to see that to follow literally the ancient line, only translating it verbally into our own idiom, is impossible. Indeed, when that sort of thing is attempted, the result is a startling negation of what the ancient Fathers of the Church were really wanting to say. In any event, we must do a more radical piece of work than such a facile exercise in the use of a dictionary. We must discover what is at stake in this or that affirmation; we must wrestle with the problem of meaning; we must look at all possible modes of restatement; and perhaps above all, we must acknowledge the tentative quality of our own manner of phrasing the "meaning which remains fructifying in the world, finding new expressions to suit new circumstances," as Whitehead put it.

4. We now come to the fourth and last of our points. Earlier I have urged that among the possible conceptualities available to us today, process thought is best suited as a tool for reconception. I said this not only because that conceptuality appeals to me by its largeness of vision, its capacity to include so much within it, and its obvious relationship to the Christian culture in which, as a matter of fact, it has emerged. I said it because I am also convinced that at the present time it is also as close as we are likely to come to the truth about things—granted always that *no* conceptuality can claim to be *the* truth, now and for all eternity.

Here I wish only to indicate once more, and briefly, three aspects of process thought that make it, to me and others, a suitable aid in our work of reconception. I shall mention *(a)* the dynamic conception of the world; *(b)* the equally dynamic conception of God as unfailingly related to and affected by the creation; and *(c)* the societal or "organismic" outlook, which is the consequence of the first two. Taken together, these three have a remarkable resemblance to the general worldview which we find in the Old and

New Testament; in this respect they are in striking contrast with many other philosophical conceptualities to which Christian thought has turned during its long history.

1. We have seen in the last chapter that in the process way of seeing things, the world is composed, not of bits of matter-in-motion, but of "energy-events," each of which is regarded as participant in a creative advance. The evolutionary perspective is dominant, leading to an interpretation of the cosmos as on the move rather than fixed and static. For each "actual entity" there is an initial aim, provided from the continuum of potentiality; the entity is then enabled by its own decision to make this aim its own, to grasp what is offered to it from prior and environing entities for this purpose, and to move towards its realization or satisfaction. No entity is without the past which makes available the materials for its initial move, but there is a novelty about the entity which establishes it as *this* rather than *that*. The environment provides opportunities which may be accepted or rejected. And the "subjective aim" of fulfillment "lures" it on toward attaining what Whitehead called its "satisfaction." Then the entity perishes, but only to provide new material for further novelty.

The procedure which suggests such a view is a generalization of concrete experience as we know it and feel it. Pondering deeply what it means to be, and to feel to be, a human being, for example, we discern just such a relation of past, present, and future, held together by some aim which provides identity. With this understanding, we can then make a large generalization. Could it be that what we ourselves know may also be true of the world at large, granted the differing degrees of conscious awareness, immediate subjective concern, and knowledgeable decision? Let us try out the generalization. If it has this wider application and if it "works" in practice, it is so far true; if it does not, we must reject it and try again. Thus there is an empirical test; but there is also the test of coherence and the confirmation by human reason—human reason here meaning not simply logical and ratiocinative capacity but also deep feeling-tones, which may be called the "aesthetic quality" of existence if we use that word in its larger Greek sense and not as referring only to the beautiful in the narrower sense.

Furthermore, we know ourselves to be living and dynamic,

much more a routing or series of becomings than a completed instance of being. Can this also be more widely applied in a generalization which is open to testing? In both instances, the process thinker believes that the generalizations are shown to be valid. Hence not only human experience is of this order, focusing past and present and future in this or that moment and moving along a path toward fulfilment; the world itself, in its smallest bits of energy, is also like this. Thus there is process throughout, a continuing process. Further, as Whitehead is reported by Lucien Price (*in Dialogues of Alfred Whitehead*) to have said shortly before his death in 1947, "The process is itself the actuality, since no sooner do you arrive than you start on a fresh journey."[19] We know nothing of some supposed absolute beginning, nothing of some supposed absolute end; we know only the process itself, in which we are participants.

2. God is no exception to this general dynamic view, for (as already I have twice quoted) he is not "the great exception to all metaphysical principles to save them from collapse, but their chief exemplification." God too is living, in a perfect degree. He too has the past, present, and future with which he deals. He supplies the initial aims for the creation, lures it by providing goals, and surrounds it with his influence which works through the various proximate occasions. He is the chief creative cause; he is also something more—which much Christian theology has declined to allow: he is the chief receptive agency. All that happens in the world, with which he is ceaselessly in relationship, has its effect upon him, increasing his joy and providing him with new opportunities for action, or diminishing that joy by denying him such opportunities. We men and women, and all other entities, exist by our prehending and being prehended, grasping and being grasped, by the various influences playing upon us or upon which we have our chance to play. God is like that, too, except that in his case he abides forever supreme in his wisdom, his employment of events, and his adaptation of them for the ends he has in view. In him all values integral to the given data are harmonized. From him the good achieved and the evil overcome by good and made into a new good are poured back into the creation enabling it, under his guidance and by his help, to move forward to newer opportunities and satisfactions.

3. This suggests that we have to do with a societal creation, in which everything is related to, influenced by, and influences everything else, God included. While it might seem that the major power exercising such influence must be coercion, the truth is that persuasion is the stronger. For you can force something or somebody to do your will in an external way, but you cannot force a response which is freely and gladly given—that can only come from the kind of persuasion which enables the other to recognize that what is sought is its *own* good. Recognizing this, decisions will be made which tend toward actualizing that good. But this is to say that *love* is the key or clue to how things go in the world; and Whitehead treasured the "Galilean vision" because it saw so clearly that this is so.

Nor (as I shall argue in the next chapter) does this minimize the fact of evil in the world. We need to see evil in a different way from the conventional one, however. Evil is essentially refusal to advance, refusal to cooperate in a social cosmos; it is self-centered contentment with things as they are; and it is willful decision for less than the true good. In us, with our human capacity to decide consciously for or against the good which is good for us and for others, including God, wrong can be devastating in its results. Not only does it damage the one who does it, as well as others and God; it also establishes a state of affairs in which right decisions are made more difficult if not nearly impossible. The final situation is tragic in the rejection of true good, the choice of unworthy objectives, and the creation of a society that is unjust, maimed, and wounded. But God handles this situation too. Out of positive wrong he can distill a good; in dealing with evil he can find ways in which a lure is still offered and a chance is given for a kind of love that is all the richer because it has faced and absorbed the sting of evil. For a Christian the story of Calvary, seen in the light of Easter victory, is the great paradigm of this pattern of divine action in the world.

There is no need to continue here with the discussion of the availability of process thought for Christian reconception. Perhaps enough has been said here and elsewhere in this book to show what the conceptuality is like and why some contemporary Christian thinkers find it extraordinarily useful and valuable in their work. Obviously the "common person" is not interested in the details of this way of seeing things; he or she is not a philosopher and has neither time nor competence to put things in this exact fashion. But I am convinced that ordinary people do in fact think this way, albeit half-unconsciously, and not least because of the diffused influence of evolutionary ideas, the sense or feeling that somehow there is a meaning in the world and in human life. They cannot easily articulate all this. But they can feel very deeply that they ought to be in some cooperative relationship with whatever purpose runs through the world, serving as instruments for that purpose in establishing a just and enriched future.

Whitehead, in concluding the remarks that Price quotes as having been said shortly before his death, had a word about this too; and with it I end this chapter. "Insofar as man partakes of [the] creative process does he partake of the divine, of God, and that participation is his immortality, reducing the question of whether his individuality survives death to the estate of an irrelevancy. His true destiny as co-creator in the universe is his dignity and his grandeur." The Apostle to the Gentiles had said much the same thing: "We are fellow-workers with God" (1 Cor. 6:1).

5

Process Theology and the Fact of Evil

In his admirable survey, *Christian Theology Since 1600,* published by Duckworth in their Studies in Theology series, Professor H. Cunliffe-Jones, lately of Manchester University, gives a brief but accurate notice of "process theology [as] a key to the understanding of God."[1] He ends this short section with a comment which is by way of being a question: "It remains to be seen whether or not theologians think that it [namely, process theology] comes too easily to the conclusion that God is love." Although he does not explicitly say it, nonetheless it is apparent that his question is raised because of his profound concern for the fact of evil and sin in the world. How can it be, we may fancy him asking, that "the dynamic nature of the universe" is "achieving integration by the mutual expression of love," when evil, in all its forms, is so obvious and so terrible a reality in that very universe?

This chapter is an attempt to show that process theology does *not* come "too easily" to the conception of God as love, nor does it overlook or minimize the fact of evil in the world and sin in human life. The point which we hope to make can be briefly summarized in these words: God is indeed love, not because we think this a good or attractive idea but because the event of Jesus Christ is sufficiently "important" (in Whitehead's highly specialized sense of that word) to be taken as a disclosure of how things really go in the cosmos, despite the terrifying presence there of the evil which seems to contradict any such conviction. The remainder of this chapter is a spelling-out of what this brief summary asserts.

I wish first to reiterate my tribute to the accuracy (and fairness) of Professor Cunliffe-Jones' brief account of process theology. Especially I commend his recognition that process thinking insists on the "living God actively responsive to the universe of his creation" and its equal stress on God's love as "grounded in the process, though its climactic expression is to be found in Jesus Christ." By thus seeing that creation and "incarnation," the given-ness of the cosmos, and the revelation of God within it, are intimately associated in this conceptuality, he has made the point which has unfortunately escaped many who write about the process view. Unlike the theologies which assume a sharp distinction between creation and "incarnation" (nature, history, human experience, on the one hand, and the awareness of and response to God self-disclosed in human life, on the other), process thinking requires us to assert that it is precisely within the context of the former that the possibility of the latter is to be found. An old teacher of mine used to put this in a telling way: "For biblical thought, revelation and redemption are not contradictory to creation but together provide a new grasp of what creation means." Elsewhere in his admirable survey, Professor Cunliffe-Jones has also stressed the disastrous consequences which follow when theology works on the assumption that these two are utterly disjunctive, for we then get an irrational or *merely* "fideistic" view of faith's convictions and a universe in which God appears to do nothing important until the moment when he steps in to redeem or repair what has gone wrong in a world from which otherwise he appears to be absent or for which he seems to have had no real concern.

This emphasis on creation *and* redemption, indeed, is the reason that the evil in the world presents so serious a question to Christian thought. If it were possible to accept some modern version of the Marcionite heresy, making a distinction between the "god" who created and sustains the world of nature and unredeemed humanity *and* the true God who is the redeemer and the savior through his revelation of love and his saving of men and women from their evil condition, the question would not arise— although even more serious difficulties would face us. But when we say, with the Bible, that he who "in the beginning" created heaven and earth is also he who "in the fullness of time" has "dwelt among us" in the humanity of Jesus of Nazareth, we are forced to reckon very seriously with all that seems to be contradictory to the "pure unbounded love" which Charles Wesley (like all Christians) saw in Jesus.

A great deal will depend, of course, on how we are prepared to define evil and sin. For many Christian thinkers, evil is a radical distortion of the created order, so much so that the world is now in the possession of some satanic principle. Talk of such "radical evil," which has often been found among the so-called neo-orthodox theologians of the present century, presumes that in some fashion the world has got entirely out of God's control. Although those theologians would never have admitted it, they tended to disregard the insistence in Genesis that the world was not only God's creation but that he found it "very good." On that biblical basis, the very worst that can happen to creation is for it to deviate from or distort the goodness which is still its deepest reality. It is impossible to speak of "radical evil" if we have understood that "radical" means "at the roots" or "basically." That sort of talk is a denial of the goodness of God's creation and a refusal to see that he is ultimately in control of it.

There are also those who, while they are not victims of Manichaeism in this modern mode, are certainly prepared to equate a realistic appraisal of the evil in the world with a pessimism that accords ill with the biblical conviction that God is "working his purpose out" and that he, and not the demonic, is supreme and victorious even now. Such theologians remind me of the words of a limerick:

> God's plan made a hopeful beginning
> But man spoiled his chances by sinning.
> We *trust* that the story
> Will end in God's glory,
> But at present the other side's winning.

Perhaps it is unfair to charge Reinhold Niebuhr, at one stage of his career, with this error. Yet his teaching that redemption is only "in principle," not "in fact," would seem to approach it. What makes the situation the more strange is that often the theologians who have talked in this vein have been the very ones who have been most insistent on the divine omnipotence. The contradiction in their thought does not appear to have occurred to them—unless, indeed, they have altogether forgotten that in Christian faith God is declared to be infinite love and not absolute power.

Let us now turn to the basic subject of this chapter and first ask, what do we mean when we speak of "evil"? In the perspective afforded by process thinking, evil is that which holds back, diminishes, or distorts the creative advance of the cosmos toward the shared increase of good. In that sense, evil is privative in nature, although it is not by any means simply a matter of appearance. The purpose of God in creation is the augmenting of all possible good, achieved through the decisions of the creaturely occasions or events. Such good is toward the satisfaction of the occasion itself, but it is also in the context which makes satisfaction for the social process as a whole a genuine potential. This means that when decision is made for self alone in disregard of others, the result will be a failure in proper advance for all, hence an evil.

Furthermore, evil comes about when in the necessary adjustment of disharmony there is a contrast too great to be subsumed in a richer pattern. Thus a violent opposition between two possible goods, leading to actual conflict, is an evil. The divine purpose is such harmonizing of various goods as shall produce a pattern that avoids (on the one hand) the tedium of monotony and (on the other) the clashing of opposites. *Contrast* is good, with the tension that follows upon it; but *stark opposition* is a potential, and may become an actual, evil. Doubtless something of this idea was in the thought of the Cappadocian Fathers when they spoke of evil in almost aesthetic terms as the ugliness that contrasts with the beauty of the created order in God's purpose.

The ways in which evil may show itself are various. There is what we call "natural evil," such as earthquakes and their consequences in suffering or loss of life; there is evil in the animal realm, including the supposedly bloody slaughter of beast by beast, with the suffering involved; there is the physical evil of suffering among men and women, including cancer and the like; there is mental and emotional anguish, which we readily see as evil. And there is moral evil which (when God is introduced into the description) becomes sin or a violation of the divine will. Here a great many different things are gathered together under one heading, although the only common characteristic is a feeling that somehow or other all these are *wrong*. This suggests that it may be useful to engage in a more discriminating consideration of evil and say something about each of the varieties commonly included under that heading.

As to "natural evil," surely it is a mistake to call an earthquake, tidal wave, tropical storm, hurricane, or volcanic eruption evil in itself. The difficulty comes when life, more particularly human life, is caught up into the situation. If an island is inhabited when it is struck by a hurricane, the disaster seems evil to us—and so it is, since human life is lost because of it. But these occurrences, as we now know, are part of the natural order of things; were it not for them, life would not be possible on this planet. We may wish that things were arranged otherwise; but as it is, they are exactly what they are called, *natural* occurrences in which it would be absurd to look for downright malevolence.

In respect to "nature red in tooth and claw," with the preying of animal on animal, we come to another matter. Here is something which seems thoroughly wrong. Yet we are told by experts that in fact there is much less needless slaughter and certainly much less pain in animal death, than our tendency to the "pathetic fallacy" would lead us to assume. I am not trying to dismiss suffering which can be very real; but there is no need to exaggerate that suffering. There *is* a considerable amount of it, largely due to need for food or protection of territory; but it would be erroneous to speak of a *vicious* quality in the animals who are thought to be most rapacious.

When we move on to physical, and above all emotional and mental, suffering among men and women, we are again in a different realm although obviously there are links with what has gone before. The suffering which we experience physically is associated with malfunction of the body, failure as we grow older for the body to keep up with the demands made on it, and warnings that we are dangerously "playing with fire" (sometimes quite literally, as when we are in peril of damage through burning), and the like. Mental anguish, with its emotional overtones, is the consequence of our capacity to "look before and after"; to experience our own and to enter into others' problems and worries and pains; and to be forced to face questions too hard for us to answer.

In all these instances, the pain which we may have to endure is the other side of the physical, mental, or emotional pleasure which we may also experience. The same "equipment" makes either one of these possible, depending upon circumstances and conditions. Finally, there is the evil of injustice, denial of human rights, and loss of genuine human freedom.

Now it is my contention that unless we presuppose a world which is a complete and finished article, something of the sort just outlined is bound to occur at the natural, physical, animal, and human levels. This is a creation which is not already made but which is *being made*. The objective in view is the only justification for the way in which it is being made; yet it is also true, I believe, that in the "being made" we ought to expect what we find— namely, incompletion and imperfection. Furthermore, while we dare not deny the reality of pain and anguish, at whatever level these are to be found, we need not attribute them to the direct will and purpose of God—unless we have succumbed to the fallacious idea that God is omnipotent in the crudest sense of the term. This is what creates the difficulty for most people, as when a mother whose child has died from some painful disease is permitted to think (even by devout Christian pastors) that it is *God's* will that the child should have suffered as it has. But what reason do we have for any such idea, save the mistaken notion that God is not only the chief creative principle in all things but is also the immediate and only cause of whatever takes place, *precisely as and how it takes place?*

Right here we need to stress the reality of the decisions of creatures, at every level from the quantum of energy up to the free choices made by men and women. Failure to stress this is failure to see that God desires, and I should add *needs,* the cooperative efforts of the creatures if his will of perfect goodness is to be effected. As Whitehead had the insight to recognize, far too much Christian theology has modelled its picture of God after the human dictator or tyrant, controlling everything with no requirement for "fellow-workmanship" on the part of the created order. But there is no reason whatsoever, save in a mistaken reading of some of the earlier material in the Old Testament, for assuming that God is like this. On the contrary, we have every reason for saying that he is so intimately related to and operative in the world, so much dependent upon the responsive cooperation of the creatures, that his plan and purpose are made actual in and through creaturely decisions and not by arbitrary *fiat* on his part.

What then is left of the notion of omnipotence? Are we arguing for a "finite God"? Not at all. Omnipotence can mean, and should mean, that God has all the power necessary to accomplish his will, *not* in spite of, but rather through, the decisions of his creation. And his infinitude or transcendence is not to be seen as absolute power to do anything, but rather in his capacity to work inexhaustibly towards the accomplishment of his purpose, with resources which are adequate to meet and overcome in the long run (and sometimes the *run* may be very long! but God has all time to work in) everything that would distort and obstruct the end which he has in view. This, I take it, is the basic deliverance of sound Christian faith as well as of the main drive in biblical thought; and it is the explanation for the eschatological note that runs through both. It is *in the end,* not temporally speaking but in the ever-present receptivity of the divine nature, that the fullness of the divine plan will be realized. Meanwhile, in the finite here and now, we have the *arrhabon,* or "earnest," of that fullness— and the person of faith lives and acts in its light. So to live is not to withdraw from the struggle against whatever is wrong with the world; on the contrary, it is to rejoice in being a "co-creator" with God (as Whitehead put it) in the creative advance which *is* the cosmic process.

When we think of evil, however, doubtless the religious person is thinking especially of sin. Here we must be careful lest we regard sin as a violation of arbitrary rules imposed from on high upon creatures who have no will of their own. Furthermore, we need to guard against assuming that the divine purpose for us is a violation of our human integrity and freedom. Sin is not a breaking of God's arbitrary *fiat* but a violation (in our freedom) of relationships with God himself and with our fellows, as well as a wrong adjustment (also freely chosen) to the natural order of which we are a part. Nor is it simply a matter of each individual. For a human being is not so much an individual as a *person,* which means that sociality or participation with others and sharing in the natural order is an integral element in the total human make-up. Hence wrong decisions, each made here and there at given times and places, can and do accumulate; and their results have consequences which affect others, nature, and the way the world goes on.

Here, I should suggest, we have the insight hidden in the traditional concept of "original sin" to describe the situation or state of deprivation or alienation in which men and women find themselves. The long accumulation of decisions which have *not* been for the wider good and for the ongoing of the cosmic movement toward good is embodied in the racial memory and deeply ingrained in succeeding generations. It produces a condition in which the possibility of right choice is reduced. Thus when we make our own decisions in this present moment, we are not free to choose with the fullness and the rightness which is the divine intention for us. The consequence is the state of affairs which Scripture describes as alien to God's will; while for each one of us there is the tragic fact of failure, due not only to our own willed selection of lesser goods (which then are actual evils, since a lesser good, in the wider context, can serve evil or wrong ends) but also to the frustrations which our concrete situation inescapably presents to us.

What *God* does in a world like this, if Christian faith is right, is to enter into, identify himself with, and suffer in the situation as a whole. He invites his children to join him in the struggle against wrong. He is not remote from the world, nor "untouched by the feeling of our infirmities" *and* by the horror of our wrong-doings, wrong-thinkings, and wrong-speakings. He is *here,* in the midst of it all, sharing with his creatures in their anguish, suffering with them in the consequences of their sin, urging them to positive action. Yet because his loving energy is inexhaustible and indefeasible, he can both accept these wrongs into himself, overcome them, and triumphantly use what happens in the creation for the accomplishment of good. Of this fact, as I suggested on an earlier page of this book, the Good Friday-Easter Day paradigm is the demonstration for the person of faith.

The reason that some have thought that process thinking slights the facts of evil and sin is simply that its way of understanding these dreadful realities differs from the conventional and traditional one. But to interpret differently the how and why of these realities is *not* to deny their presence and their horror. A confusion seems often to be found when it is assumed that unless the usual view is adopted the facts which that view was concerned to stress are neglected. This is an absurd error, however understandable it may be.

In an article published long ago in *The New York Times Magazine,* the American writer Paul Goodman wrote these words: "If the chaplains"—he was speaking specifically about undergraduates and their contact with religious faith as commonly presented on college and university campuses—"would stop looking in the conventional places where God is 'dead' and would explore the actualities where perhaps he is alive, they might learn something and have something to teach."[2] What Goodman said in respect to one particular situation may be more widely generalized. The difficulty is that in much conventional Christian thinking God is wrongly conceived. He is "looked for" in the wrong places; and hence problems are created which would never arise if one looked for him in "the actualities" where he is alive and at work.

It is my contention that these places, where God is indeed alive and working, are in any and every movement, personal and social, historical and natural, where good is being sought and accomplished and where men and women work for justice. This means that it is an error to think of him in the total process as uniformly and equally operative—in the bad and the good, the hateful and the loving, the ugly and the beautiful, the wrong and the right, injustice and the truly sound concern for righteousness. He is not the cosmic manipulator of a system in which everything, just as it is, directly reflects his purpose and expresses his will.

Thus we return to the basis of Christian faith in the event of Jesus Christ. It is the venture of that faith to assert in word, but above all to enact in deed, the centrality of the clue given in that event. This clue is the disclosure of love (or persuasion, if you prefer the Platonic word) as the nature of the divine whom men and women worship. The history of religion is the story of the way in which this affirmation has gradually come to be accepted as the truth of things. Not only in Christianity but elsewhere, this movement is to be seen, as Dr. Trevor Ling has well demonstrated in his fascinating portrayal of *Religions East and West.*[3] But in the event of Christ, seen as the strikingly vivid and compelling disclosure of love in act (bringing to concrete actuality the insights of philosophers and seers, sages and prophets, of all times and places), the affirmation of Love—here given a capital "L" because *cosmic and divine* love is in view—comes through with such clarity, and awakens such wholehearted response, that it may be taken as indeed "important" and normative. Here is no sentimental love, but strong and invincible Love-in-act.

Such Love, cosmic and divine, is made visible in human loving, in the One who "had loved those who were his in the world, but now he showed how perfect his love was" (John 13:1)—to the extent of total identification with them to the point of death. The conviction that this death was not to write *finis* is the deepest significance of the Resurrection. Being what he was and doing what he did, "death has no power over him any more" (Rom. 6:9), and is shown triumphant over it, as over all that is evil, by God's act in "raising him from among the dead."

The source and enabling power of the Christian faith that God is love is found there. It is not come at "too easily," but with full recognition of all that would seem to contradict it. In that sense, the truth of Kirsopp Lake's saying is demonstrated—that faith is "life in scorn of consequence." It is a life lived on the basis of the moral certitude that "God in Christ was reconciling the world to himself" (2 Cor. 5:19) and that he was doing this by a sharing in the evils which, through creaturely decisions that distorted and obstructed his will, were yet not able finally to thwart that will. God, so known, can even make man's wrath, as well as whatever other evil there is in the world, "add to his glory" (Ps. 76:10). And this glory is not self-congratulatory satisfaction but the widest possible sharing of all creatures in the goodness which is his purpose and which is also his own innermost nature.

6

Suffering and Love

We now turn to a more detailed discussion of human suffering as seen in a process context. Almost all discussions of suffering concern themselves with what we may style its negative side; very few of them speak of the positive aspects of suffering. In taking this approach they are undoubtedly dealing with the subject in the way in which it presents itself to most of us, certainly when it is felt as a "problem."

The typical questions are, "How can we reconcile suffering, which is a bad thing, with a loving God?" and "Why should there be such unspeakable suffering in a world that is ordered toward the achievement of a good end?" Thus suffering is usually classified with natural catastrophes, disease, moral wickedness, and the like; it is placed at once in the category of *evil*. For the traditional theist such evil requires a theodicy—some way to justify "God's way with men" and with the world. The atheist is in a different position, of course, since he or she does not think about a good God who in some fashion is pre-eminently the causal agency in the world but on the contrary assumes that the world is an aimless process, even if a mechanically ordered one. For the atheist evil is a fact, not a problem. Yet my observation leads me to think that for the atheist too the negative aspects of evil, and particularly of suffering, are the more frequently considered.

Among the few treatments of suffering which have recognized the positive side, the most suggestive in recent years is a brief essay by Professor Daniel Day Williams, entitled "Suffering and Being in Empirical Theology," in *The Future of Empirical Theology.*[1] I have learned much from this essay and it has considerably influenced my own thinking; I wish here to call it to the attention of the reader of the present book.

Before we turn to some significant positive points in respect to suffering, however, it is important to insist that the reality, the horror, and the evil quality of suffering are not to be minimized. There is always a danger that those who wish to stress the positive aspect of some subject will minimize the negative aspect. This is in no sense my own position. Suffering is rightly included in the class of things evil. And I am not distinguishing in this chapter between "physical" and "mental" suffering, however real and important this distinction is. Some of the points which follow are obviously more relevant to one or other of these two aspects of human suffering, but the two belong together in our experience. For most of us suffering is the way in which evil makes its presence felt most obviously. If it is not our own suffering, it is that of another— perhaps a person we love, perhaps people about whom we hear, or about whom we read in newspapers and books or whom we see on television. Suffering is *bad*.

We dare not adopt the stupid notion that it is simply the result of our ignorance or failure to be "in tune with the infinite" (a phrase used in a North American religious group which rejects evil as an objective reality). Such attitudes are flippant as well as absurd. So also is the idea that suffering is a matter of psychological states only and can be "put in its place" if we have healthy thoughts. This latter position is related to the one just mentioned; but it is also to be found in supposedly Christian circles which have overstressed "mental health" and "positive thinking." To all these dismissals of evil one can retort with the limerick:

> There was a faith healer of Deal
> Who said that pain wasn't real;
> But when I sit on a pin
> And it punctures my skin,
> I dislike what I fancy I feel.

In other words, if physical suffering is nonexistent and is only a mistaken idea in the human mind or a psychological aberration, the fact remains that the mistaken idea and the psychological aberration are *very* real—*that* at least is no "fancy."

We are called upon to do all in our power to alleviate suffering. We are not to think that because suffering can have a positive and constructive value it is therefore to be allowed to persist in any situation and for any person where relief is possible. It is incumbent upon us, whether we are Christians or humanists, theists or agnostics or atheists, to reduce suffering so far as we can.

Finally, while we shall discover that there is a deep truth in the traditional Christian teaching that "our suffering is to be offered to God," we dare not use this as a facile way to condone or commend suffering, either for others or for ourselves. That would be blasphemy. Unhappily some Christian ascetical manuals show an almost sado-masochistic strain which suggests that it can be *good* to inflict pain on others and *salutary* to inflict pain on ourselves, in each instance as a "way to develop character." That suffering *can* develop character is true enough; but to inflict it or induce it is to do the work of the devil—and this is all the more appalling when it is thought to be a proper way of responding to a loving God.

Let us assume, then, the reality of suffering as a plain fact, our duty to alleviate it, and our refusal to inflict or induce it for any one, including ourselves. With these assumptions firmly understood, we shall look reality in the face and not attempt an escape. Only then can we presume to speak positively. Thomas Hardy's lines say just this:

> If way to the better there be
> It exacts a full look at the worst.

In what has been said so far "the worst" has been looked at. Is there any "way to the better"? In other words, what positive statements may we make concerning suffering and its constructive contribution to human experience?

I shall suggest and comment on the following: 1. Suffering can deepen our understanding of life in this world. 2. Suffering can purify our motives and desires. 3. Suffering can enrich our relationship with others, both through greater sensitivity to their inner experience and through providing us with opportunity to assist them. 4. Suffering can enable us to grasp more profoundly the nature of God as "cosmic Lover" who shares in suffering because he identifies himself with his creation.

1. *Suffering can deepen our understanding of life in this world.*

The Roman poet Vergil, in one of his lovely "half-lines," writes *sunt lacrimae rerum:* "tears are present in the things of life." For whatever reason, there *are* "tears" in human experience, whether they actually be shed or whether they belong to what Wordsworth had in mind when he spoke of "thoughts that do often lie too deep for tears." There is a sadness in life, partially accounted for by its brevity and uncertainity. We are here for but a short time and we shall not pass this way again. Awareness of transience and impermanence can either bring us to snatch each moment and drain from it the last ounce of pleasure, or (if we are deeper persons) force us to think again of the mystery of life, tinged as it is with anguish even if also suffused with joy.

Just here suffering has its contribution to make. If Vergil could speak of the "tears in things," we can all testify that there is pain in our most profound and enriching experiences. Human existence is intended to be a life in love; and love is not a matter of superficial good cheer. A Spanish proverb speaks of the "suffering of the lover," while still another tells us that "making love is declaring one's sadness." Folk-wisdom often sees more truly into the heart of things than the cleverness which we tend to admire but ultimately find shallow; and folk-wisdom as represented by those two Spanish sayings tells of the inextinguishable sorrow and suffering in human existence. Life is not high comedy nor farce; neither is it unrelieved gloom. It is *tragic*—that is, it presents us with suffering which we must either endure in Stoic fashion or accept in a willingness to learn more about how things really go in the world.

I have called this chapter "Suffering and Love." Anyone who has loved truly and profoundly will testify that suffering is integral to genuine love. There is the pain of physical separation from the beloved one; and there is also the other nonphysical kind of separation which mysteriously divides the two who love. They are united, sharing life together; yet at the same moment there is the "I" and the "Thou" which provide not only the necessary distinction (so that the relationship is not sheer identity, which would not be union at all) but also the painful knowledge that we *two* are not now and never can be completely and fully *one.*

Presumably it is this suffering in love which accounts for the famous Wagnerian aria *Liebestod.* But Wagner did not under-

stand the real truth of the matter. He would have his hero and
heroine so lost one in the other that their love was but death to the
identity of each. That is not the case with real love, where the two
are not *lost* in their union but are each of them *found* and given a
new life in communion. Yet Wagner's music about "death in love"
would not have had popular appeal if it had not pointed, however
mistakenly, at an aspect of life which most men and women know
very well. Even physical suffering can help us understand that life
is short, broken, and unfulfilled; and that it yearns for completion. We live in the midst of broken dreams, broken hopes, broken aspirations, broken desires, broken lives. The barriers which
life sets up between us and others are *not* broken down by any
natural creaturely force; only *God's* love, identified with us in our
suffering humanity, "has broken down the barrier" (Eph. 2:14).
We can be held by that love even when we are in exquisite pain.

2. *Suffering can purify our motives and desires.* Our greatest
sin is our pride. We tend to think of ourselves as "the monarchs of
all we survey." Suffering can bring us to our senses. It can make us
humble and force us to see that we are not the center of the world,
nor do all good things depend upon us. Indeed suffering *means*
"being acted upon"; it means that something is happening *to* us,
over which we have no control and which we must accept in bitterness *or* in humility. If we do the former, our bitterness will turn us
into a source of infection for others, because bitterness is like a
disease which is caught from the presence of those who are af-
flicted by it. If we do the latter—accept inescapable suffering in
humility—we can become persons who see that they live in a social world, much of it beyond their controlling, and that only by
accepting this and working against wrong can they find any enduring peace.

Suffering resembles what as children we were told were
"growing-pains." Positively accepted without bitterness, it can
help us to grow. It can purge us from base ideas and ideals and fit
us for better and more shareable ones. Patient endurance is not
easy, but it *is* possible; and endurance, with the patience to see the
thing through for good or ill, is strengthening and (if I may use a
word that sounds far too "idealistic") ennobling for us. The man
and woman who has not suffered, mentally or physically, is likely
to be superficial, to think that things can come to them without

struggle and pain, and to assume that when they do not get what they want it is somebody else's fault, never their own. People like that live only on the surface of life.

We are told in *Hebrews* that he who was "the leader who would take them to their salvation" (Heb. 2:10) "learned through suffering" (Heb. 5:10). Here "suffering" presumably includes more than pain; it is probably best translated as "experiencing." Through what Jesus experienced, both in ordinary daily life and also through his anguish of heart and pain in body on the Cross, he *learned*. So do we. The men and women whom we admire as great persons are those who have thus learned through experience, have purified their motives and desires because of that experience, and have come out on the other side, in triumph over "the changes and chances of this mortal life."

3. *Suffering can enrich our relationship with others, both through greater sensitivity to their inner experience and through providing us with opportunities to assist them.* Perhaps because of the pride which is our greatest sin, perhaps because of failure of imagination, we are all too often insensitive to other people. Obviously they are *there* and we must take account of them; but our attitude toward them and our ordinary relationships with them can be superficial rather than penetrative of their inner selves. They are external to us; we are external to them. This failure in imagination and sensitivity is part of "man's inhumanity to man"; it allows us to be indifferent, when not callous or cruel, to the experience of other people.

But one of the positive results of suffering, whether it be physical pain or mental anguish, is to open us up. In a mysterious way we realize that men and women are bound together in a community of life—and that community might well be described in words first used I think by Albert Schweitzer, "the fellowship of pain." To know suffering in ourselves makes us aware of the truth that others know suffering too; and when we know that, we have entered into their lives, if only a little way. Furthermore, we can share suffering in another fashion as well, since nothing can open us to others, or they to us, so quickly as the communication of our experiences of loss, deprivation, and pain. To share in these, even by talk about them but above all by action to overcome them, is to share in real inner human experience. When I suffer I know what it is for others also to suffer. I can "sympathize." Then I am impelled to do all that is possible to provide for those others some relief in *their* suffering, to support and care for them.

4. *Suffering can enable us to grasp more profoundly the nature of God as cosmic Lover who shares in suffering because he identifies himself with his creation.* What has been suggested in the previous three points may be carried to the cosmic level. I understand life in the world in its tragic dimension; I know myself better and am enabled somewhat to purify my motives and desires; I can enter more profoundly into the experience of others and assist them in their suffering. What in my finite and creaturely way is possible is only a pale reflection of what God always is and always does. He knows the world in its tragedy. He does not need to purify his motives and desires, for they are abidingly pure and right, but he does need to relate them to the world and its ongoing process. He is related to his creatures in sympathetic identification with their inner experience and the outward happenings of their lives; and he is constantly giving them the help they need as they move on in their human pilgrimage. Which is to say that God is love.

The *kind* of love which God is, however, must be distinguished from the sort of benevolence which would "do good" to others but exists in a certain detachment from them. For love to be true love it must not only give but be ready to receive; it must not only talk but be prepared to act. It is here that the process perspective about God, adopted in this book, is enormously valuable. We humans learn that truth from our suffering, since we are brought to realize our dependence upon others. God does not need to learn this, because God *is* this. His love is "pure unbounded love," in the fullest sense of giving and receiving, of mutuality, of comradeship and participation. Indeed, it is the "love of God made visible in Christ Jesus our Lord" (Rom. 8:39): not dispassionate and aloof, but involved and caring, up to the point of death, on behalf of others. In such a fashion *God's perfection* is manifested; and it is in our own suffering too that we come to understand, as philosophical speculation finds it difficult to do, that perfection is not unchangeable and unrelated "absoluteness," but the inexhaustible capacity to give, to receive, to be related with and influenced by (as well as to influence and affect) others in a great cosmic society. Perfection is not self-subsistent and self-contained; it is nothing other than active love. This is God's nature.

It is possible for any sensitive human being to arrive at some such conclusion. The history of the great religions demonstrates this. In the fascinating study of world religions, *Religions East and West,*[2] to which we have already referred, Dr. Trever Ling has demonstrated with a wealth of illustrative material that in Hinduism, Buddhism, and Islam there has been a slow but persisting movement of thought from ideas of deity which stressed "absence," or impersonal absoluteness, or coercive power, toward a concept of deity in which tenderness, comradeship, identification, compassion, and active love are given the central place. The story of Judaism and Christianity, taken as a single movement in human history, is not utterly atypical; it is a concentration or focusing which provides both insight and motive for the interpretation of all human awareness and deepens and enlarges the vision of how things are and go in the world, and how we humans can play our part.

Some may think that to say this is equivalent to denying to the divine self-disclosure of which the Bible is the record, its distinctiveness and speciality. But this is a misunderstanding. If by speciality we mean that there is an absolute chasm or abyss separating other human instances of religious and moral awareness from the specifically Judeo-Christian position, then of course we have made such a denial. But there is another possible and much better meaning of speciality. It can be used to indicate a definitive, because peculiarly vivid and clear, disclosure of God to his children. In that case, what is declared in the biblical disclosure is no contradiction of what has gone on elsewhere, but (in William Temple's words) a "correction and coronation," a fulfillment and completion, of all those other glimpses, hints, intimations, and responses to divine activity and presence.

This second position is simply a modern phrasing of the view found in the early Apologists, in the Alexandrine Christian Fathers, and frequently in the mainstream of Christian thought. Only in a few, like Tertullian in the ancient Church (and even then with certain qualifications), do we find an entirely negative attitude toward the development which Dr. Ling has demonstrated. The Patristic doctrine of the *Logos* "spermatically" or partially present in all men and women but specifically active in Jesus Christ, is one instance of this more generous, and I should claim more profoundly Christian, attitude. The speciality of the Christian affirmation of God as participant and suffering Lover is not utterly anomalous but is effectual in awakening, as no other disclosures seem to do, the response of intense, all-inclusive faith and action.

My final comment returns to the conventional pious admonition that we are to "offer our suffering to God." This can be a dangerous bit of advice, as I said earlier. Yet it is the expression of an inescapable truth. For we can offer to God *everything* we are and have and do and experience; this is our way of saying "Amen" to his doings. Human existence, our deepest faith tells us, is meant to be *ad maiorem dei gloriam,* given to God and to his greater glory. God's glory, however, is not some extravagant display of pomp nor the overwhelming manifestation of power. That would be to identify it with the "glory" of an earthly ruler. God's glory is his love in action, his sheer goodness. To offer ourselves to promote God's glory is to make available to him the little we have done and can do in our mortal life, thus providing him with material that he can purify and employ as he works ceaselessly in love, in and with his creation. In that context our experience of suffering can be offered to him in the certitude of faith, knowing that he will receive it and make it a part of his continuing advance, as he gives himself to his children for their own greater good—which is his greater glory.

7

Prayer in Process Terms

It would be no exaggeration to say that for vast numbers of our contemporaries, prayer has become a meaningless enterprise. There are many reasons for this. The practical necessities of life in a world like ours, with its excessive "busyness," make it difficult to find time to engage in prayer. The antiquated forms of prayer found in many service-books and in many guides to personal devotion make prayer seem outlandish and an affair of olden days without much relevance to our contemporary situation. The slow waning away of traditional Christian belief, thanks both to pragmatic factors and to increasing knowledge, provides no context for the exercise. But basic to this difficulty about prayer, in my judgment, is the theological and philosophical problem which it seems to raise. In this brief chapter I shall attempt to look at the matter from the perspective of process theology, which avoids many aspects of that problem.

A brief summary of that theology, here repeated, will suffice to give the proper setting for what will follow. Process theology, as we have seen, is the interpretation of the Christian faith through the use of the conceptuality worked out initially by Alfred North Whitehead, the Anglo-American philosopher who died in 1947; and later developed by Charles Hartshorne, the American philosopher, and by others in North America, in Britain, and in Australia; and then employed by Christian theologians who find in it an appropriate and valuable instrument for making sense of Christian affirmations about God, humanity, and the world.

Those who think in a process way are prepared to take with utmost seriousness the fact that we live in an evolutionary world; that "becoming" is more basic to that world than "being" or "substance"; and that there is an ongoing creative advance such that novelty appears within an overarching continuity. The world is "composed" of occasions, each with its "initial aim" given it by God from the continuum of possibility, each with its "subjective aim" which is the initial aim accepted and sought along a specific routing. Each occasion or energy-event is also continually grasping, and being grasped, by the other energy-events of which the cosmos is composed—in the technical term, there is a "prehension" which makes each entity a creative cause of itself, although always in and under the chief creative cause that is God.

Thus we have an ongoing movement marked by dynamism and by sociality. Because each occasion influences and is influenced by every other occasion, there is no such thing as a self-contained and entirely self-existent being. The way in which this is worked out is for the most part through lure or persuasion, although force has its role to keep the cosmos from straying too far from its intended goals. Yet *love* is the dominant motif; and this is as much true of humanity as of God. God is himself "pure unbounded love," whose nature and ways of acting have been disclosed supremely, says Christian faith, in the event we name Jesus Christ; and human existence is being created to become a creaturely lover, in God's image and after his likeness. This means, too, that in human existence social belonging, or sharing, or mutuality, is a necessity. To seek self-centered goals, to refuse to advance with the world and one's fellows, to rest content in partial achievement, is the wrong about human life which religion has called by the name of "sin." And "redemption" or "salvation" means to be grasped by the divine Love and Lover, so that we become "co-creators" or (in Pauline phrase) "fellow-workers" with him in his continuing purpose of goodness widely shared and richly enjoyed. I have already argued for this understanding.

So much for the general outline of the conceptuality provided by process thinking—a position which many will find similar to the views of Pierre Teilhard de Chardin as outlined in *The Phenomenon of Man*[1] and *The Divine Milieu*.[2] Although Teilhard read only one book of Whitehead's, and Whitehead knew nothing of Teilhard, there is often a remarkable similarity between them, perhaps this is another illustration of the truth that "an idea finds its time and its exponents." What we have to do with here is a conception of the world as dynamic and social. And we have also to do with a model of God in which he is seen as both intimately related to and influenced or affected by the world in which he acts.

But there is one other point to be noted. In what Whitehead calls God's "consequent nature," God takes into his life, he values, and he uses for his purpose of greater good, whatever has been achieved in the creation. He does not, because he cannot (being himself Love), assimilate or appropriate the evil and wrong; but he can and does extract all the good which it contains or which it can make available; he can make everything turn to God's praise, which is to say to his greater enjoyment and expression of sheer love.

Now prayer can be put in this context of process thinking; and when it is put in that context, it makes sense. That is what I wish to urge and explain in the remainder of this chapter.

In a view of the world where everything is already finished, or a view in which God already knows all that has happened and does happen and will happen, or a view in which there is sheer determinism with no room for freedom—in such a world prayer is meaningless. Why? It is meaningless because the whole course of events, including the human mind and its thinking and desiring and willing and hoping, has already been absolutely established. There is no chance for any human wish or desire or aspiration or hope to make the slightest difference; all is fixed and determined and the best that could be done would be simple acceptance of a *fait accompli.*

But in a world which is open to creative advance, with the possibility of genuine novelty, things would be different. Furthermore, in a world where one energy-event influences all other such events and where God himself is affected by what happens in creation, in a world where God accepts and uses that which happens (including the happening of human desires and hopes and aspirations), there is every reason to affirm the possibility that prayer (rightly understood) can be effectual. It is *this* kind of world which process thought, building both on our knowledge of what we see and experience and also on our own deepest intuition as to the significance of human existence as a *felt* reality, provides for us. And such a picture of the world is scientifically accurate, so far as we can know it; it is also a view that is "religiously available," in that it makes room for the religious response of men and women in adoration, in discipleship or "fellow-workmanship," and in prayer.

Yet the prayer must be the *right sort* of prayer. Far too often it has been assumed that prayer is either an escape from the world into heaven, in which case it is not supposed to affect anything save the one who prays, or an attempt to persuade God to do what otherwise he would not do. But genuine prayer is neither of these. The great "masters of prayer" have always insisted that true praying consists essentially in two aspects: "raising of the mind to God," on the one hand; and on the other hand, earnest and adventurous affirmation addressed to God that his will shall be done, and that it shall be done through the one who is praying. The New Testament shows Jesus in the Garden of Gethsemane as praying in exactly this manner. We might say that true prayer, in the Christian sense, is both active passivity and passive activity.

It is the former, because it is the wholehearted dedication to God of the believer's life and existence; it is the latter because it is a willingness to be used by God so that the divine purpose may be accomplished more effectively and completely. Thus all Christian prayer is "in the name of Jesus Christ," which is to say that it is in his "spirit" or in the attitude and manner which his whole life and teaching, as reflected in the New Testament material, implied and expressed. It is a tragedy that so much of the teaching about prayer which has been given to the laity and which the clergy assume to be proper, is a denial of this basic Christian understanding. Prayer then becomes a silly attempt to coerce God and the more people who are brought to pray for something, the more God is obliged to do it or give it! Or it is an equally silly effort to run away from the hard and harsh facts of this world. When neither of these is found to "work," prayer is given up as meaningless—and no wonder, for such prayer *is* exactly that.

When I pray, I adore God as the "supreme excellence" and I thank him for his goodness "which endures forever." I acknowledge my own wrongs and ask for reintegration into his ongoing movement of love. But I *also* speak of the things that, in my ignorance as a finite being, I think to be both good and according to his will. I may be mistaken about this; yet in asking I add my own tiny desire, tiny yet as strong as I can make it, to his enormously great desire and action for that good. God can *use* that; and without that finite desiring he would not have at his disposal one of the genuinely effectual causative agencies in the creation. Having it, he is able to make it serve purposes which are his own and which in being his own (by definition of his character as love-in-action) are also those best for his creatures as he intends and seeks for them to become.

We learn more of what is according to God's purpose of love as we pray in our ignorance for what we assume to be good and right. Thus we are enabled to "grow in grace," to see that ultimately it is what a Prayer Book collect calls "increase in faith, hope, and charity," which is our greatest need; to add our willing to the divine willing; and in this way to respond to the divine call to "work together" with God, who (as St. Paul says in the letter to the Romans) "by turning everything to their good, cooperates with all those who love him" (Rom. 8:28).

8

The Approach to Christology

For many of us one of the attractions of process thought is in its general compatibility with the biblical portrayal of God as "the living God," of the created world as dynamic and open to the divine action, and of human life as being made "toward the image of God" so that human existence may be brought both to reflect and be the instrument for the divine purpose. Of course, we should not wish to employ that conceptuality if we did not also think that among the viable possibilities open to us today it is the most satisfactory. No responsible process thinker would wish to claim that it is *the* truth, since there is an inbuilt safeguard in the conceptuality against any such extravagant assertions. Nonetheless, we are sure that if *some* conceptuality, with its general philosophical categories, is necessary in the theological task, this one is the most suitable among those now available; and the fact that it is to a very large degree compatible with the scriptural witness is an added, perhaps even the chief, commendation of it.

In this and the following chapter, I shall hope to indicate some of the main emphases in a process way of looking at the person and work of Jesus Christ. Here certainly is the crucial case in point, since for any theology which is genuinely Christian what is said about Jesus Christ is both central and decisive. Furthermore, what is said about him must include reference both to his relationship with God and to his genuine identification with human experience. The Christian tradition has consistently maintained that in some very real fashion there is in Jesus Christ an interaction of God and human life, however varied may have been the ways in which this has been expressed at one time or another in the history of Christian thought. In what way, then, does a process approach portray this interaction, this double relationship? And is that way adequate to the deliverance of Christian experience as, in their responsive faith in Christ, the company of believers are sure they have been enabled to enter upon a genuinely "new" manner of seeing, understanding, and coming into contact with God, as well as knowing "newness of life" (Rom. 6:4) as brothers and sisters of him who called himself "the Son of Man"?

I do not propose here to argue the case for theism of some sort. Suffice it to say that I regard those who think that we can retain some real discipleship to Jesus *without* a theistic reference as entirely mistaken. Someone has characterized certain contemporary "theologians" (if that is a possible name for those who deny *theos,* or God) as people who say, "There is no God and Jesus is his Son." That is, such thinkers seem to take it for granted that even if there is no reason to talk about God, there is still every reason to "take one's stand with Jesus," to use words employed by one representative of this school. All sorts of questions may be put to people like that. I shall not put them here because many others have already pointed out the inconsistencies, absurdities, prejudices, and ambiguities in such a stance. I must repeat, however, that when we were told that "God is dead" we should have inquired *what* "God" it is about whom such a statement was made. For nobody can use the word "God" without having in mind some concept of deity. My own conviction (as I said in earlier chapters) is that persons who spoke in this manner about God's "death" were in fact telling us that certain concepts of God (perhaps very hallowed and traditional ones) had "died on them." And rightly so, I have said, in respect to some of these concepts: God pictured as sheer being itself or unmoved mover or cosmic dictator or moral tyrant or unaffected (and hence impassible) reality subsisting entirely without, or apart from, relationships. All these concepts I take to be "idols," as Whitehead put it, with little if any possibility of reconciliation with "the God and Father of our Lord Jesus Christ," and hence with no claim upon Christian allegiance, no matter how many distinguished theologians have accepted them and sought by ingenious logical legerdemain to reconcile them with the "pure unbounded love" which Jesus (and the basic Christian insight) affirms to be the divine, worshipful, supreme, and unsurpassable reality we would name when we say the word "God."

It will be helpful to repeat here, but now in very summary form, some of the major emphases of process thought, as they relate to our conception of God and his ways in the world. I do this because of their christological importance, as we shall see in the sequel.

1. Process thought is insistent upon the dynamic, evolutionary, or "processive" nature of everything known to us. Things do not remain fixed and static; they are on the move. To understand anything, we must see "how it goes"; and there is nothing in our experience which is not "going somewhere." This should not be taken to suggest that there is an inevitable and inescapable *progress*. A process theologian is often obliged to urge readers and hearers to remember what any dictionary makes quite clear: that process or change is not equivalent to improvement. Put simply, you can "proceed" to hell quite as readily as to heaven! The point about process thinking is simply that "going" is the basic character of the cosmos—and, I add, of God too if God is truly the "living God."

2. In such a picture, the "stuff" of the cosmos is not a collection of substantial entities to which things happen. The basic realities are what Whitehead called "actual entities" which are focusings of event or happening. Out of the past, possibilities are presented for the continuing of the movement and for new developments or novelties; but these are not *things*. Every "actual entity" is a richly complex organic whole in which past occasions lead to this or that focal concrescence (or making concrete) of drives, thrusts, movements, occurrences. You and I are not substantial "selves" (although we are indeed "selves," but in a different sense from the old "substantialist" idea). We are a focus of happenings and our awareness of our identity does not involve some *thing* to which are attached, adjectivally, the happenings which we experience. In different fashion but with analogous interpretation, everything in the world is to be conceived as an "energy-event," forming part of a "creative advance" into novelty or genuine newness.

3. It is apparent from what has been said that another basic characteristic of the world, as process thinkers see it, is its societal or "organismic" quality. Everything affects, and is affected by,

everything else; "no man is an island entire unto itself," nor is anything else in the creation. We influence everything else; everything else influences us. There is an interrelationship or interpenetration by virtue of which each actual entity "prehends" or grasps past entities and is itself "prehended" or grasped by succeeding entities. The whole creation is a movement or thrust of creativity, in which events are the "building blocks" (and what an inadequate and misleading image *that is*!—but a better one is hard to find) which are being used, but in which those "blocks" are always mutually interactive and related. God too is related to everything else; indeed, for process thought God is the supreme instance of such relationship, rather than subsisting in some supposed isolation from what is going on in the world.

4. Finally, the insight of process thought is that coercive force is not the dominant *motif* in the cosmos, nor in God, although much theology has assumed this to be the case. The dominant motif, the basic quality, the deepest and most real (and also the strongest) undergirding and directive reality, is *love.* Whether we use, as Whitehead did on occasion, the Platonic notion of "persuasion" or whether, as a Christian will wish to do, we talk about "love so amazing, so divine," the point is the same. Coercion is indeed necessary to prevent valuable and necessary contrast from becoming finally destructive conflict, and to prevent freedom for decision in every reach of the cosmos from becoming anarchic chaos. Yet the essential nature both of God and of his "agency in the world" (in Whiteheadian language) is nothing other, nothing less, nothing more, than *sheer love.*

Of course, we must be clear that by love we are not speaking about sentimentality, sloppy toleration of anything and everything, or superficial emotionalism, but rather of strong, demanding self-sacrificing, self-giving; we are speaking about mutuality, or gracious receptivity, and the like. Furthermore we must be prepared to take very seriously the obvious deviations, backwaters, negation, anguish, injustice, suffering, and wrong in the world—all that the word "evil" denotes and connotes. But process thought is better able to handle that issue than the so-called "theodicies" where God is regarded as so much sheer power that he is inevitably made responsible, either directly or permissively, for such evil as there is.

So far, then, we have a brief summary of the chief elements in process thought as they are relevant to Christian theism and above all, for the purposes of this chapter, to the significance of the person and work of Christ.

From what has been written above it is evident that a process Christology cannot be stated in terms of "substance." We must work in another way. That is not to say, however, that the *intention* of classical Christology once stated in such "substance" idiom is to be rejected. The great theologians of the Church have always been obliged to use whatever conceptuality was available to them; and we should not denounce our predecessors in the Christian faith simply because they used "substance" and similar notions and tried to work out their doctrine in those terms. How could they have done otherwise? What we can say, however, is that *we* need not use that kind of conceptuality if we have available to us another which is more compatible with the way in which the biblical witness portrays God, the world, and human existence.

The biblical witness speaks about what God *does* and only through his *doing* comes to conclusions about what God is. Indeed, if we follow the Whiteheadian statement discussed in a previous chapter, "that a thing *is* what it *does*," we are coming very close to the scriptural "I shall be what I shall be"—meaning that what I do (here God is represented as speaking, of course) will be the manifestation of what truly I am. For the Bible, God is indeed transcendent, in that he is inexhaustible, as he is unexhausted, by his *known doing*. There is always "more" in God than that which we see of him in his observed activity. But the "more" is not a static "isness" but a dynamic *life*, utterly faithful to his purpose of love and laboring unceasingly and indefatigably to fulfill that purpose in the world. And the world is no mechanical affair nor is it an aggregation of static things. For the Bible it is open to God's action upon it, capable of response to that action either positively or negatively and with genuine freedom; it is plastic to his purpose yet able to defy and hence interfere with the implementing of that purpose. We humans are also marked by freedom of response. The Bible tells us that we are "made of the dust of the earth" upon which God's Spirit has breathed to make us living and conscious creatures; and because of this we are enabled either to respond to

God so that we become personalized instruments of the divine will (which is always *chesed*, mercy or loving-kindness) and thus achieve or receive *shalom* (or fulfillment and harmony) *or* to reject God, under whatever form God presents himself, and so move toward negation, denial, loss of true human selfhood, and hence toward what is symbolically called "damnation."

The biblical story is the tale of God's disclosing himself to his human children as they were able to receive and grasp what he disclosed. So it was that to the Jews he was first known as sheer power, revealed in natural marvel, in violent storm and earthquake and volcanic eruption, and in warfare and strife. But then came Moses and the earlier prophets who saw that God's power was not *sheer* power but rather (to use some famous words of Matthew Arnold's) "the power that makes for righteousness." For the prophetic insight, that was what God disclosed himself to be. Yet this was not the end, for later prophets (Hosea, parts of Isaiah, Jeremiah) were enabled to see and to proclaim that the divine righteousness was not abstract justice, but nothing other than the accepting *chesed* to which we referred a few lines above. God was essentially loving-kindness and mercy, ready and eager to receive his children's faithful response and make available for them *shalom* or abundant life. His power and his righteousness must be interpreted in terms of that *chesed*.

The coming of Jesus, summing up what had gone before, brought a new—yet not without intimations and hints earlier and elsewhere—self-disclosure of God as Love. In the historical event of Jesus Christ—including what prepared for it, the occurrence itself with its reception by his contemporaries, and the consequences in the experienced "presence" of the "risen" Lord in the community of faithful, responding discipleship—God was now seen as what I delight in styling the receptive and responsive cosmic Lover. As such, however, he not only accepts and receives his human children's response; he goes out preveniently to awaken that response. He is like the loving father with the prodigal son, the shepherd in search of the lost sheep, or the woman sweeping the house to recover the lost coin. Jesus *taught this*; what is more, he *enacted this* in his concrete activity. Above all, his whole existence, from his birth through his death and resurrection, *was a placarding of this before the world*. However partial and uncertain may be the story of the details of his historical career, *this* is what it revealed; and it was to *this* that the first Christian community gave itself in utter faith, in adoration, and in discipleship. Indeed, it was *this* which knit the first Christians together in a fellowship "in the Holy Spirit," grasped by and impelled to respond, as such a fellowship, to what God had done toward them, for them, and in them.

What has just been said has two corollaries which require attention. The first is that we recognize honestly that we do not possess in the New Testament the sort of material which will permit us to know the "Jesus of history" as if he were the hero of a biography or a novel, psychological or other, and then from this work out a Christology which will depend for its validity on an analysis of his supposed subjective experience or on a summary of the details of his supposed teaching. What we *do* find in that material is the *fact* of Jesus presented in terms of the response and witness to his impact, mediated through the faith which that impact occasioned. Tillich used to speak of "the biblical Christ"; he employed this term to indicate the picture which emerges when we take the whole New Testament witness with great seriousness but without attempting the impossible task of discriminating between what can be said with absolute certainty to be historical fact and what is the deliverance of the primitive faith in the figure who was preached and believed. We have to do with a credible witness, not with a precise historical narrative.

As we have seen earlier, Whitehead warned against "paying God metaphysical compliments." Here I wish to warn against what I shall call "moral compliments" paid to the historical Jesus. He was not an "admirable Crichton" (to use the title of Barrie's play about an omniscient and omnicompetent butler); he was a man of his own age and place, who thought and acted in terms appropriate to that time and place. He shared in the culture of his own people; he was a Jew and can only be understood in a Jewish context. The consequences for Christology of this more intelligent way of looking at him will include an understanding that he did not think as we do, but that like every other human he was caught up in the relativities of the historical situation which was his. The fact that, like Prometheus in the ancient legend, he brought the divine fire to those who were caught up into his action is our sufficient justification for taking him, as Christian faith indeed always has taken him, to be a signal disclosure of God in human terms.

A second point which demands attention—and discussion at some length—is that all talk about faith in Jesus is by necessity expressed in language of a mythological sort. But to recognize this does not make it meaningless or absurd or incredible. *All* religious language has that quality. It is appropriate, therefore, to say something here about a fairly recent controversy in theological circles, symbolized by the titles of two books, *The Myth of God Incarnate*[1] and *The Truth of God Incarnate.*[2]

The word "myth" need not mean, what many people seem to take for granted, a story that is not true but rather is pure fiction or illusion. Obviously the word is frequently used in that sense; but it is plain enough, from Plato's use of the Greek equivalent *muthos* as signifying "a likely tale," that a myth may or may not be true in the sense of "literal" historical fact—whatever *that* may mean. Here I cannot pursue this very important question about which far too little has been said or even considered. Furthermore, what is meant by "truth" in such a context is equally problematical, once we get beyond the usual trite assumption that it means simply "what is so." In what sense can something "be so"? That is still another difficult problem, as any philosophically informed person will know.

However, I wish here only to insist that no theologically instructed person, certainly no professional theologian, can think that the "truth" about such a matter as the activity and presence of God in a human life can be stated in literal, prosaic, or univocal language. Religious language is always allusive, analogical, symbolical, indicative, not absolutely precise and exact (as we suppose, perhaps mistakenly, that scientific discourse must be). On the contrary, there was great wisdom in the remark once made by G. K. Chesterton when he was discussing religious faith: "Don't believe in anything that can't be told in painted pictures." Religious language, when it is most profound and illuminating, is invariably imaginative in quality. Coleridge saw, and said, just this many decades ago. It may very well be the case that it is exactly in "the myth" that "the truth" about Jesus Christ is being said.

Much of the discussion which the two books I have mentioned

seem to have aroused appears to me to be based on such a misunderstanding as must arise from a supposed contradiction between these two words, "myth" and "truth." Those who appear to have been most disturbed by the "myth" book—granted that they *read* it, which from much of the material in the correspondence columns of the religious press seems doubtful—include some who have a far too simple, not to say simplistic, notion of "truth." Others, of course, are simply the victims of the idea that all "myth" is "fairy-tale." It is unfortunate that the contributors to the "truth" book seem, with some honorable exceptions, to fail in this respect too.

The basic issue could be put very simply and in this way: What are we saying, or what are we trying to say, when we declare (as a matter of our Christian faith) that "Jesus Christ is Lord"? What do we mean when we assert, from our own experience and from that of the centuries of Christian faith, that in him "God has visited his people, he has come to their rescue" (Luke 1:68)? Surely the language of the latter biblical text is of a symbolic or if you will a "mythological" sort. But what is it getting at? Or even more simply, what *is* this affirmation about the event which we name Jesus Christ telling us as matter of a religious conviction?

I must try to answer that question. But I shall first comment on the odd tendency, found again in much that has been written and said about these two books, to identify *the words* we must use to point to any conviction with that conviction *itself*. Far too many assume, it would appear, that the verbal statements or propositions which have come down to us from the past—say, from the age of the Fathers—are in and of themselves the reality with which faith or conviction is concerned. But surely it is or ought to be obvious to any thoughtful person that the value of any statement or proposition, however hallowed by age, is to be found in the way in which it points, or fails to point, to the reality in view. Long usage certainly makes a certain reverence desirable and even (I should say) necessary; but it does not and cannot establish that particular statement or proposition as eternally valid. Thus we are forced back once again to the question: What do we *mean* when we say such things? Or in still another phrasing: What is christological talk trying to get at, trying to say?

Unlike some suggestions in the "myth" book, I believe that

"incarnation language" may very well, and probably should, continue to be used, in appropriate places, about this christological assertion; and the reason for this is chiefly to affirm our historical continuity in the faith. But if the word "incarnation" is taken in the sense that in Jesus, and in him alone, God is "incarnationally" at work in the world, then the language can be very misleading. Among other things, it may seem to deny the pervasive activity of God elsewhere in the creation and among his human children. I have noted in an earlier chapter that when the ancient Fathers were faced with the question of God's more general activity, they found a way of dealing with it; they talked about the *Logos* in his wider revelatory and salvific action and they set *Logos sarkotheis* ("the enfleshed Word") in Jesus in *that* context. St. Athanasius in the *de Incarnatione* explicitly declares that precisely because the cosmos *as a whole* is the *organon* of the Word, we can see in Jesus a definitive and specific *human organon* for that same Word. Again, if it is thought that the word "incarnation" or the phrase "God incarnate" must be understood in a precise Chalcedonian sense, that carries with it the corollary that the philosophical presuppositions with which the "Definition of Chalcedon" was framed must also be accepted as irreformable. As it happens, for a great many of us those philosophical presuppositions are no longer meaningful. Despite the arguments of Brian Hebblethwaite in the "truth" book, that a "substance" interpretation of things is theologically necessary, we must reply firmly that belief in Christ as Lord is not so tied to such a philosophy that rejection of the latter presumably must be also rejection of the former. This is absurd. Were all the Antiochene theologians, all those who in non-Mediterranean lands thought and talked in the "dynamic" idiom of Syriac theology, and everybody since that time who has worked with a philosophy of "act" in developing a Christology, entirely heretical just because they did not, or do not, employ "substance" idiom?

I believe that what is at stake here, so far as Christian faith is concerned, is the enduring conviction of the Christian tradition as a whole—a tradition which we inherit, into which by baptism we have been incorporated, and in which as believers we stand—that *God is active*, in some decisive and definitive fashion, in the Man Christ Jesus. Further, this activity of God is so much in unity with the activity which was Jesus' as a man, that we may rightly say

that there, in that place, at that time, in that event, we are given
the clue to what God is always and everywhere up to and also the
clue to the significance of human existence itself. To say that, we
must use language that is available to us. *All* of it will have a
symbolic, analogical, poetic, yes a "mythological" quality. For
even talk about "divine activity" is not straightforward literal discourse. How could it be, when it is men and women like us, finite,
ignorant, defective as we are, who are using it?

In the "myth" book Michael Goulder suggested that we should
talk not of "unity of substance" but of "unity of activity of God
and Jesus." He said that "if a Greek word is wanted" it should be
homopraxis, which in his view would be better than *homoousia*.
Yet even if we accept this, as I do, we must also recognize that we
still continue to use language which is not literal but suggestive
and symbolic.

It is not very important that we should be able to work out in a
neatly defined fashion just what gave rise to an "incarnation"
view of Jesus as Christian faith responded to him. Goulder's own
idea of an influence from Simon Magus and the Samaritans seems
pretty farfetched; in the "myth" book Frances Young does better
with her study of the quite varied origins and differing developments of christological definition. But neither of these get at the
main issue. That issue for us is just this: can we still assert that
God is initially active and continuously at work in the event of
Christ? Can we still assert that in that event a genuine and complete human existence is the means for expressing what God is
doing? And can we still affirm that in the total event God and
man are in some serious sense co-active and hence co-present?
The last point, incidentally, follows if what has been urged before
in this book is true as the Whiteheadian conceptuality would say,
"A thing *is* what a thing *does*." This, by the way, is a very biblical
sort of assertion.

Professor Macquarrie, in the one contribution to the "truth"
book which takes into account such considerations as I have ad-
duced so far in this chapter, urged that "at least three things" are
implied when we speak of "incarnation": (a) that "the initiative is
from God, not man"; (b) that God is "deeply involved in his creation"; and (c) that "the center of this initiative and involvement is
Jesus Christ." That way of expressing it is pretty close to the suggestions that I made in the last few paragraphs. But surely it

would be entirely possible to accept, *con amore,* Macquarrie's and my points; and yet at the same time opt for what Professor Wiles has styled (in a perhaps not too happy phrase, since the adjective he uses suggests *minimizing,* which is not his intention) "a *looser* meaning" of incarnation. What he means by this is that it is more meaningful and even more faithful to see the abiding Christian experience of Jesus in the context of the wider divine self-disclosure in the world, than it is to take what he calls the "more precise" meaning, which would see this disclosure as confined to Jesus alone rather than see it as defined in Jesus. The traditional "definition" of the person of Christ at Chalcedon, taken as it stands, along with its use in much subsequent theology, is unhappily likely to make Jesus an utter anomaly and not the decisive and classical expression of God's revelatory and salvific activity in the created order.

In my opinion there was much wisdom in the insistence of Dr. J. F. Bethune-Baker, one-time Lady Margaret Professor of Divinity at Cambridge, that we benefit greatly by retaining old terms like "incarnation" (not to mention others like "atonement" and "sin" and "grace"), while at the same time we benefit from our newer knowledge, wider experience, and (maybe) deeper grasp of the insight of Christian faith. Hence, he said, we can seek to expand the significance of those terms. If we cannot do this we are in a sorry state. More importantly, we shall have "frozen" our Christian thinking by our impossible reactionary response to that which the Spirit may be teaching us. We need both continuity *and* newness.

Professor Maurice Wiles has put in moving words what he calls the "cash-value" of christological affirmation: "It is supremely through Jesus that the self-giving love of God is most fully expressed and man can be caught up into the fullest response to him. . . . The power of God was set at work in the world in a new way through his life, ministry, death, and resurrection."[3] Thus, he goes on to say, Jesus remains "the personal focus of the transforming power of God in the world." He then adds that the "traditional incarnational language and imagery would seem appropriate as a pictorial way of expressing these truths." Surely he is right; yet it *is* a "*pictorial* way"—and here I recall Chesterton's remark quoted earlier in this chapter.

I have said that we can and probably should continue, on the proper occasions, to use the traditional word "incarnation," provided we give it an extended meaning. Yet it should be evident that we are not required to "have faith in the Incarnation," as some of those who have discussed these two books have said. "The Incarnation" is, after all, a human concept. We are to have faith *in Jesus Christ*; which is to say, we are to commit ourselves to him in his disclosure, through concrete human existence, of the reality of God. Through him we have been given a disclosure of God; from him we have received what we know to be wholeness of life (or in traditional language, redemption or salvation); in him we have found a center for living and an imperative for action. But there is no reason why some other term than "incarnation" might not have been found, or might not still be found, which would state all this. If I had to suggest one, I should say "God's focal self-expression in a full and genuine human life." This brings us to the final and more constructive side of the matter, which will be treated in the next chapter. But before we turn to it, something else needs to be said here.

In his *Song of David*,[4] Christopher Smart wrote about what God has "determined, dared, and done" in Jesus Christ, crowning all else that he has been doing and still is doing in nature and among humans. To speak in that manner is to speak in the imaginative, allusive, poetic idiom which is natural to all deep religion. In a way, it is to return to the picture language of Scripture. Thus what in one sense is "myth" is also a statement of "truth"; but it is truth said in a fashion appropriate to the matter in question. Nor does it fall victim to Professor Macquarrie's fear that an "idealistic world—view" may be substituted for "fact." Jesus is not to be taken as "primarily the historic exemplar of the eternal truth of the unity of God and man," which is the notion that Macquarrie fears might be suggested. On the contrary, since our world is a world of concrete events, each of them with its own speciality and each with its own "importance" (in Whitehead's phrase), there is here no vague generality. Rather there is a quite particular window into the nature and activity of the personalized and personalizing thrust in the cosmos which is the hither side of the transcendent mystery we call "God."

What has been said in the last few pages is no more than my

own suggestion for a christological approach which will make sense today. Let me end this chapter by saying that the controversy over "myth" and "truth" need not have happened (although probably it has been therapeutic for us that it *did* happen) if all of us had concentrated our thinking on faith in Jesus Christ himself. Then traditional or contemporary concepts, statements, propositions, and words about him would not have been given more importance than is, in fact, proper to them.

9

A Process Christology

How then can we work out a Christology which will be adequate to the experience of God's revealing and redemptive activity in Christ? The height of the New Testament interpretation is probably in the Johannine text, "The Word was made flesh, he lived among us" (John 1:14). But I think that we can do better just now to take the Pauline words, "God in Christ was reconciling the world to himself" (2 Cor. 5:19). Both texts are getting at the same point: namely, that "the Self-Expressive Activity of God" (which is what "the Word" means in the Johannine text) is operative in Jesus Christ by employing instrumentally a full and genuine human existence, in a Man who actually lived among us in order to bring "grace and truth" (divine favor and the very reality of God himself) to his human children and thus to "reconcile" them to himself in a full, free, loving, obedient relationship in which he can really *be* their Father and they can really *be,* and *act as,* his sons and daughters in *the* Son—*filii in Filio,* as the Fathers of the early Church put it.

"God in Christ was reconciling," that is to say, God was *doing something* in that historical and human event. The Pauline text is not so much concerned with the *how* of God's "presence" as it is with the *what* of God's activity. We have here a clear instance of the general Scriptural stress upon God's energizing in the historical process; anything said about matters like "presence" must be a subsequent concern. As a matter of fact, with the process perspective in mind, we can put it even more accurately if we say that God's activity *is* his presence. It is not as if God took up his abode here and *then* went on to "do something"; it is the plain fact that when and as God acts, he is by that very acting "present" in his creation. To take the former position would be to fall back once again into the fallacy of "substantialism" with happenings adjectively attached to "substance"; whereas to adopt the latter position is to be in accord with the stress both of process thought and of the main trust of biblical witness.

Hence we can put the resultant christological view in a straightforward fashion: in the historical and human event of Jesus Christ, who was a Man among human beings at a particular time and place, there was an activity of God which was marked by the quality of speciality and which was a decisive moment in the long story of God in relationship with his world. Or in even briefer words, in Jesus Christ there is a human activity—since he, like all humankind, was a routing of events to be identified as *that* Man—*and* a divine activity, since God was "working his purpose out" then and there in a distinctive and particular way.

This means that there was a genuine union of human activity and divine activity. In classical Christology, as we may recall when we consider again the Chalcedonian definition adopted A.D. 451, the data which are put forward for consideration are precisely these three: *(a)* God; *(b)* Man, or genuine human existence; and *(c)* the effective union of the two. The way in which the three were affirmed at that great Council was of course by the use of the accepted Greek substance-philosophy. Hence it was asserted that Jesus Christ was "of the same substance with the Father, as touching his Godhead," "of the same substance with us as touching his manhood," and that the two were "united" in a fashion which was described by the use of the famous four "Chalcedonian adverbs": "unchangeably, unconfusedly, indivisibly, and inseparably." The divine and the human in Jesus Christ were always to be seen as "distinct," since each remained what it was; each was not to be "confounded" with the other; yet the divine and the human were inseparable since the union was neither incidental nor accidental, but integral, organic, and abiding, in accordance with the divine purpose and by means of a prevenient divine act which evoked a freely responsive human act.

This statement of the data for Christology is of enormous value to us, even today. I have said that we cannot accept the philosophical categories which were used by the Church Fathers; indeed, few things are more pathetic than the effort to continue to employ those categories when there is honest recognition of our entirely different ideas about "how the world goes" and "what God is." When that sort of effort is made, we have an unfortunate and fatal confusing of categories. We are mixing up types of discourse, with the result that we do *not* succeed at all in saying what those Fathers intended. To say the "same thing," in the sense that we seek to reaffirm the intention or thrust of their position, demands that we shall not confuse categories nor mix styles of discourse, but do something much more important. Our task will be to find ways in which, with the use of such categories and such discourse as we today naturally accept, we shall say once again that in the historical and human event of Jesus Christ, *God* is at work through a genuine *Man*—and this in such a manner that the Godhead and the human life in Palestine, and that same Christ "risen from the dead," are really, abidingly, and integrally *one* in the total historical activity which we name when we say Jesus Christ.

It is just here that process thought comes to our help. If the basic reality of the cosmos is dynamic, with events or "energy-events" as its "stuff," and if there is an unfailing interrelationship among and between all such events, then it is not impossible to glimpse how there can be such a union as we claim to see in Jesus Christ. Furthermore, if God is himself related to everything else, and is affected or influenced by everything else (without for a moment ceasing to be supreme, unsurpassable, and worshipful—and hence abidingly God), then there is always and everywhere an interpenetrative activity between God and the creation. Not in Jesus only but throughout the entire cosmos there is an "incarnating movement"—God comes to us as he acts in and with that which is not himself. Also what is not God has its effect upon God, who respects his creation in its creatureliness, its finitude, its creativity, and its freedom, and therefore accommodates his ways of working to that which the creation is able to accept, receive, and employ. Of course there is an *over-plus;* God is not identical with the creation; he is more than and transcendent over it. But he is not its contradiction. He does not need to intrude, as it were, from "outside," in order to work within it, since he is unfailingly operative there; without him it would not "exist" at all in the patterned and purposive form such as we know.

In principle, the so-called "Scotist" view is right—that is, what happened in Jesus Christ is the "implied goal and center" (as Baron Friedrich von Hügel once put it) of what God is everywhere and always "up to." Here, in this concrete instance, we have the disclosure of God for what he is doing in the world and hence for what he *is*. Had we not fallen into wrong (had we not "sinned") the same final purpose would have been worked out. But on the other hand the so-called "Thomist" view is also right—that is, since we have in fact fallen into wrong (we are "sinners"), what God does in Jesus Christ is necessarily for us the provision of a way in which his creative purpose cares for and provides a path forward that is available to erring and defective humankind. This redemption is not merely a repair-operation, in which God alters his purpose and rescues his children from the sin into which they have "fallen," as if God's plan had been so imperfectly worked out that he was obliged to adopt an entirely different program. On the contrary, redemption is a new act within the continuity of the total creative advance vis-à-vis human existence.

Through this activity in Jesus Christ, those who hitherto by their free decision have for millennia opted to follow their own self-centered, self-regarding, and easily attainable goals, are given both the truth about their situation *and* the "grace" to "turn around"—after all, repentance is *metanoia* or "change of mind" with a resultant change of direction for living—and having "turned around" to follow the path which in the divine intention has always been theirs: toward their becoming "in the image of God," and thus toward reflecting and acting for the divine purpose itself.

This is indeed a radical "turning about," given what we have made and continue to make of ourselves in defiance of the purposed goal set by God for his human children. Because of the millennia of wrong decisions, communicated through our societal interrelationships, we are in the situation in which alienation and estrangement are *almost* "natural" for us. Not quite completely "natural," however, since something of God's purpose still remains in us; we have lost the divine "likeness," but (despite what some of the Reformers said) we have not been deprived of the divine "image." Admittedly this assertion rests upon a mistaken exegesis of Genesis 1:26; and Luther and Calvin were quite correct in pointing this out as an error in the tradition beginning with

St. Irenaeus' treatment of the text. But false exegesis may be a path to true understanding. Here, in my belief, the error in interpreting the text points toward a truth which experience (and, I believe, sound Christian understanding) of God's ways in his world confirms. There is still "that of God" in God's children, as the Quakers say, in spite of and in contradiction to their sinfulness. Hence redemption is not a "rescue-expedition"; it is a "restoration" to that which God purposed. That way of putting it seems unfortunate, however, since it talks in language which does not sufficiently take account of the inevitable ongoing of the world. It is better to say that in Christ God makes available the grace, the strength, and the loving will to live now and hereafter in accordance with his abiding intention for his children.

But now we must ask: *How* can the divine activity and the human activity be so at one that we have to do with an "unconfused, unchanged, indivisible, and inseparable" union? My reply rests upon still another insight of process thought. Once more I must refer to its stress upon *love* as the basic motif in God and in the creation. Only if we take such love with utmost seriousness can we come anywhere near grasping how the uniting of the divine activity and the human activity could occur. I am urging that love is an ontological category, if I may put it thus. Far from being an adjectival quality modifying something else, far from being a "second word" to be used after we have *first* talked about God as *esse a se subsistens* or *ens realissimum* or "being itself," love is the very root of deity. It used to be said that aseity (or self-existence with no relationships to others, self-containedness so that such relationships are incidental) is God's root-attribute. I wish to insist that love, not aseity, is the root-attribute of God. Even more, I wish to insist that love not only is an attribute of God but *is* God. Or better phrased, since we must use personalizing language about deity (because God is in communication with others, himself aware and self-aware, free in his action, and integrated as a unity in his existence), God is what I have earlier called "the cosmic Lover," and the cosmic Lover is God.

We have said that every human existence is being created to become a lover—to live "in love with the brethren." That is to say that we are being created to become, we are becoming if we will allow this to happen—and human freedom is essential here—

creatures who are to live in love and to live also in *Love,* where I again capitalize the initial "L" in the second use of the noun "love" to show that it is *in* God that we are intended to live. This is God's purpose for us. If Paul Lehmann is right in saying (in *Ethics in a Christian Context*)[1] that God's "purpose for man is to make him and keep him human," we must at once add (and Lehmann would accept this gladly) that to be human is to be "in love" and "in Love." In other words, the intended relationship is love. The divine Lover and the human lover are to be at one, so that each lives in the other, God in us and we in God.

With this background, we can see how in the historical and human existence we name when we say Jesus Christ there *is* a union of God and that existence which is indeed "unconfused, unchanged, indivisible, and inseparable." Our difficulty has been that we have been using the wrong models in our discourse about "how God and man are united in Christ." We have been talking about two "substances" which simply cannot be *united* since they stand over against each other and the only way to bring them together is to give one or the other the dominant place, so that Jesus becomes either God disguised to look like a man *or* a Man who is supremely inspired by God—*not* the One in whom God and man are *really* united, with each remaining itself and each doing its "proper" work. Or we have been talking about two wills, conceived in each instance as coercive agencies, which again simply cannot be united save by an overruling of one by the other. Here there can be no genuine integral belonging of one *in* as well as *with* the other. Then Jesus becomes a Man who was obedient to God's will *or* his human will is overpowered and lost in the divine will. Or finally, we have been talking in terms of two "consciousnesses," in which once again there can be no real union, but only a human consciousness illuminated by God *or* a divine replacement of human consciousness by the divine "mind."

If we reject all these and similar models and instead talk in terms of love, we are speaking in a different idiom, and in one which makes it possible for us to see a genuine union without the reduction or negation of either of the two who are united. God is Love; he is the cosmic Lover. Human life is defined as "becoming a lover"; it is being made to respond in answering love to the initiating, prevenient, out-going Love which is God himself. The analogy of human love comes to our assistance; and it is surprising that while practical religion among Chrisitan people has always talked and thought and lived in this way, generally theologians have been unwilling or afraid to let it be the clue in their task of making sense of that practical religion. This has been a tragedy; we might even say that it has been an appalling instance of apostasy from what Whitehead styled "the Galilean vision" of God as Love itself, the cosmic Lover himself.

The human analogy is sometimes distrusted because our human experience of love is so limited, deficient, even sinful. But if Jesus, as represented in the Gospels ventured to use human analogies to speak about divine realities, some of us would dare to think that it is entirely proper for his followers to do so as well, provided that they guard themselves carefully against reading human defects into the divine and provided also that they recognize that any human analogy must necessarily be inadequate to God and to God's ways in his world. Therefore I am now going to use the human analogy of love shared among us and known to us as we enter lovingly into another's life and open ourselves to receive love from another. This is our best (and dominically validated) insight into God's relationship with his human children, supremely in the instance of Jesus Christ his Son and our Brother.

First of all, in human loving there is what I style a prevenience in love. Someone moves toward us in love and that movement awakens in us the response of love. This coming to us in love gives what a Whiteheadian would call "an initial aim." That is, to know oneself loved is to be given a purpose in life, toward the realization of which we thereafter exert ourselves. We know that we are loved; therefore we strive to live in response to such love, to make ourselves genuinely recipient of it, and to express this response in our daily life. Furthermore, when we are thus loved we are aware of a continuing and faithful lure or attraction which surrounds us at every moment, evoking from us a constant desire to give more of ourselves to the one who has first loved us and to do what is pleasing to our lover. We are enabled to do things that seemed incredible or impossible. We discover depths in ourselves which we never knew to be there, precisely because the love wherewith we are loved has revealed them to us or evoked them from us. We move onwards to an ever-deeper realization of the relationship of

love, so that more and more it becomes true that we live in our
lover and our lover lives in us. We seek always to do what Kierke-
gaard called "the works of love," as our grateful response. In the
end we trust that we two shall indeed become "one," yet without
for a moment damaging or reducing or destroying the integrity of
our own respective selfhoods. Far from that happening, each of
the lovers becomes more a real self in the union which exists between them.

There is no possible relationship in human experience which is
deeper, more all-embracing, more fulfilling, and more demanding, than that which we have just been describing. This is human
life at its finest and best. To live in love is truly *to live:* as the
recusant poet Robert Southwell once said, "Not where I breathe,
but where I love, I live." Everything about us, including our
bodies as well as our minds and spirits, our materiality as well as
our spiritual capacities, our acts as well as out thoughts, will be
included. It is not with my mind or spirit alone that I love—I love
with my whole being or I do not really love at all. What this might
suggest about human sexuality and its truest meaning is another
matter which we need not pursue here. It will suffice to say simply
that our sexuality is also included in our loving, even when it does
not seek specifically "genital" expression; all friendship, for example, has a sexual context and content in this extended sense of
the adjective "sexual."

Now let us apply this analogy to the union of God and human
existence in Jesus Christ. God is prevenient to the manhood of
Jesus; it is God who gives the "initial aim" to the manhood in that
Man—and if the divine activity in love is to bring us to itself in and
through Jesus Christ, then this establishes the speciality and decisiveness of what God is "up to" and is doing in that place. At
every point in the existence of Jesus, the divine activity is operative, not in contradiction to the humanity nor in rejection of any
part of it but in and through it all—in teaching, preaching, heal-
ing, comforting, acting, dying, rising again. The divine activity is
continually at work; and the human responsivity is continually
present through the entire existence of the Man Jesus. He is then a
personalized instrument for "the Self-Expressive Activity of
God," "the Word," just because he is also utterly responsive to
that which God purposes and to what God is doing in and through

him as a Man. And because he *is* a Man, "he learns through what he experiences," as the Epistle to the Hebrews puts it.

This response can be no automatic affair, as if Jesus' manhood were a puppet pulled about by the strings of the divine puppeteer. No lover and the beloved are related like two substances nor like two striving wills nor like two consciousnesses; their relationship is deeply personal and personalizing. It is a matter of give-and-take, mutuality, with the giving as free as is the willingness graciously to receive. Here is nothing mechanical, static, nor artificial. On the contrary, here what we sometimes call "moral characteristics" become deeply ontological ones.

So it was not strange for the Antiochene theologians, especially Theodore of Mopsuestia, to speak of marriage as an analogy for the union of God's activity and human activity in Jesus Christ, nor to speak of God's being in and with Jesus "as in a Son"—the "well-beloved One" in whom God is "well-pleased"; and therefore to use the Greek words *eudokia,* or exactly such "good-pleasure" in the Beloved, and *synapheia,* or precisely true personal and personalizing union, in affirming God's action (and hence presentness) in Jesus Christ. I hope that I may be permitted to quote here what I have written elsewhere: "The most complete, the fullest, the most organic and integrated union of Godhead and manhood which is conceivable is precisely one in which by gracious indwelling of God in man and by manhood's free response in surrender and love, there is established a relationship which is neither accidental nor incidental, on the one hand, nor mechanical and physical, on the other; but a full, free, gracious unity of the two in Jesus Christ, who is both the farthest reach of God the Word into the life of man and also (and by consequence) the richest response of man to God."[2] Or as Dr. John Robinson has put it, "There is no contradiction between a man 'living' God and God 'living' a man."[3]

But what about the "self" of Jesus? Was this human or divine or some mixture of both? The answer to this question is to be found in a proper understanding of the meaning of selfhood in the relationship of love. I have noted earlier that in process thought the notion of a "substantial self" cannot be entertained, for that would be to introduce a *thing* (however supposedly "spiritualized") into our discourse. Rather, "self" is the word we use for the conscious awareness of our identity, through which the past which has gone to make us up, the present relations in which we stand, and the future goals toward which we strive, are held together in a serial or processive unity. We reason, will, and feel as such selves. But it is not as if we *had* a brain or a mind, or a body or a heart. We *are* all these together in a complex organic unity; and the divine intention is for us to be on the way to wholeness, however defective this may be at any given moment in and among us finite, erring, and human creatures.

The "self" of Jesus, understood in such terms, must have been a genuinely human self. If this were not so, then his full and true humanity would be denied; and the Church has always wished to insist on such a full and true humanity, however inadequate may have been the language in which this was done. On the other hand, God too is a "self," in that he is the personalized Love which is transcendent to, yet operative in, the creation, with his own awareness, freedom, purpose, communicability, and relationships with others. Again it is love which gives us our clue.

In the loving relationships of two people, such as we ourselves know—finite and defective as we all are—both selves are involved, both are included, both are active; yet neither one supplants the other. The union of the two in the deep communion of love makes possible a true unity which is two-ness in one-ness. In Jesus, then, we have a human self that was open to, the agency for, and responsively acting with, the divine self: that is *how* "God is 'in' Christ." Or in our earlier manner of putting it, the two activities, "the Self-Expressive Activity" (that is, the Word or *Logos*) and the human activity which is proper to our own existence are at one, intimately, deeply, mutually. "I am in the Father and the Father is in me" (John 14:11), Jesus in St. John's Gospel is represented as saying; hence he can also be made to say, "The Father and I are one" (John 10:30). In the Fourth Gospel this is not formulated in precise triunitarian terms, but its sense is clear enough. The mutual indwelling of the prevenient divine Lover and the human responsive lover establish a unity which is full and rich, complete and effective. There can be no more adequate nor complete union between God and human life than such a one, in love and in Love.

We now turn to some related matters: *(a)* the "uniqueness" of that which was by God "determined, dared, and done" in Jesus Christ; *(b)* the question which naturally follows from this in asserting the "finality" of Jesus Christ; and *(c)* the way in which all this fits into a triunitarian understanding of deity. To each of these we can give but brief attention, but about each of them something must be said if this discussion is to be adequate to its subject.

1. Some misguided Christians have assumed that they honor their Lord when they insist that he is to be regarded as what I have called elsewhere "the supreme anomaly"; they think that those of us who would say that he is "the classical instance" are reducing him to the level of "any man." This is nonsense. First of all, there is no such thing as a "mere" man or a "mere" woman; each and every human existence is peculiarly itself, however many may be the parallels and continuities it has with others. Once more, process thought comes to our assistance in its view that each and every "actual entity"—and hence each and every "routing of occasions" such as your life, my life, anybody's life—is marked by its own special focusing of prehensions or "graspings" which establish it for what it is. Nobody is identical with anybody else; each has his or her own particular quality.

But more than this must be said. What was done, and continues to be done, in and through Jesus Christ is an indication that there is indeed genuine speciality (as we say in Britain; there seems to be no exactly equivalent term in North America)—that is, it is itself and nothing else. In this sense it may be called "unique," but the word is a dangerous one if (as is usually the case) it suggests a removal of Jesus from the context of human existence. If we are to use the word at all, we had better follow Professor C. F. D. Moule, a colleague of mine in the divinity faculty in Cambridge, who has spoken of a "uniqueness of *exclusion*" as a nonbiblical notion and a "uniqueness of *inclusion*" as the intention of Scripture when it talks of Jesus. Jesus Christ includes, not excludes, all that is truly human; he defines, but he does not confine, the ceaseless working of God "for us men and for our salvation." If he were entirely different, he would be entirely meaningless to us. Because he is "one of us," yet distinctively himself in what he was called to accomplish, he can be both our Brother and our Lord and Savior. It is his being "one with us" that makes it possible for him to bring *us* newness of life or redemption; it is because he is distinctively himself that it is truly possible for him to do just this.

The assertion that he is "the classical instance" of what God is always doing does not diminish his importance in any way, if we have the right idea of what such a "classical instance" means. It increases his importance. If somebody speaks of general truths—such as, God is always and everywhere bringing his children to live in love and in Love, to the degree and in the way that they can accept this and act upon it—what we have is exactly a *general* truth; and general truths do not have much cutting-edge. We are likely to say, when told of such a general truth, "All right, maybe that is so; *but show me an instance.*" In Christian faith, Jesus Christ is the *instance.* He does not contradict or deny whatever we may know of God elsewhere and otherwise; God does not refuse his gracious work for his human children until and unless they have met Jesus Christ, the Man of Nazareth. On the contrary, in Christ he makes it clear, in a vivid, compelling, signal, and effectual fashion what he—the cosmic Lover or God—*is always doing* for his children. And hence he enables us to make a response of equal intensity.

In attempting to make this point clear to students I have often used the illustration of a library reading-glass. Take it out into the sun and turn it so that it will catch the rays which beat down upon, say, a college garden. Those rays are bringing warmth, health, brightness, and beauty to everything in the garden. But when they are caught, focused, intensified, concentrated (use whichever word you please) in the glass, they bring about a quite remarkable result. For a piece of paper or cloth held beneath that glass catches fire. I do not wish to press the illustration, which in any event is too impersonal; but it will perhaps help to show how Jesus Christ can indeed be "the classical instance" and *also* the bringer of life-giving salvation from the meanness, ugliness, and wrongness of human existence—that is, salvation from our sinful situation and our sinful deeds. Because in him the initiating divine Love met full and obedient human response in a human loving, something happens to those exposed to and caught up into "his life." Their "loveliness," as a hymn puts it, can be established, replacing the lovelessness which marks most if not all our existence. Thus Jesus is special and decisive for us.

2. But is he "final"? Much depends upon the meaning we give

that very ambiguous word. If we intend it to be a way of saying that Jesus is the *end* ("there won't be any more") in God-human relationships, then the New Testament itself contradicts us, for Jesus is said to have told his disciples that there is "more" to come (see the "Table Discourse" in St. John's Gospel, 14–16). But if we intend "final" to mean what above we have styled special and decisive for us, we are talking in an intelligent and intelligible way. I have said that Jesus does not confine God but defines him in his way with his children. Thus to define *is* to be "final" in the second meaning of the word. Here is the clue, the key, the disclosure in act, of what God *really* is "up to" in the world and thus what God *really* is as God. Nothing could be more "final" than that! Yet this "finality," like "uniqueness," is *of inclusion,* not exclusion. For us he is at the center; the circumference is anywhere and everywhere, when and as men and women are enabled in whatever way to meet the divine Lover, who surely can be trusted to do for them the very best that can be done. As we have seen, in Whitehead's word used in a quite different connection, there is "importance" here; which is to say, here we have the instance which tells us what the cosmic story is all about and what part we are to play in its continuance.

In the early days of the Church, the great theologians had their own ways of putting this. They spoke of the *Logos,* or Word, of God who was universally present and at work, but who in Jesus was (as they believed) visibly placarded before the world. They said that "the Word was made flesh" in him, although always that same Word had been "the true light that enlightens all men" (John 1:9). And this brings us to the last of our three related topics.

3. In the developed theology of the Church, the triunity of God has been asserted. This has never meant that there are three "consciousnesses" in God, as some modern theologians have inaccurately asserted. The word "person" is a poor English term derived from the Latin *persona* to translate *hypostasis,* which means in Greek something like "abiding way or mode of being and doing." Talk of this sort is not "condemned" Sabellianism, which had to do with three *temporal* modes, not with abiding and enduring ones. God is *una mens,* one mind, said St. Augustine, speaking with the whole biblical witness behind him; Christians are in no sense polytheists, even in a sophisticated theological sense of the

word. There is *one* God. But "the Self-Expressive Activity of God," God himself as he acts in his creation, is there too; supremely and signally "the Self-Expressive Activity" has come to human expression in Jesus Christ. So Christian faith declares. There is still more. The event of Christ, as "the classical instance," has evoked a response. This response is indeed human but its compelling quality, its highly personalized manner of declaring itself, and its capacity to raise us above our usual and ordinary human level of acceptance and consequent action, have led Christians to assert that here too *God* is at work. Not simply in the Christ-event with its special quality of response, but at any time or place where creation is brought to conform to God's purpose of creative love, God is at work enabling and assisting the entirely free creaturely response. This is the Holy Spirit's doing, say the Christian centuries.

But "a thing *is* what it *does*," as we have often quoted from Whitehead on earlier pages. Thus the deepest insight of Christian faith is that God in the mystery of his own selfhood is not a solitary monad but richly personal and hence richly social. To be a person in the modern sense *is* to be social; personality and sociality are the two sides of the same coin. God is in continuing relationship with the world; and this is reflected back, so to say, into the very life of God himself. Many Christians would perhaps prefer to say that the relationships God sustains with his world are reflections of an immanent relationship in his own life. At any event, He is best symbolized for us as "Three in One," not as sheer and unqualified singularity. Here too, by its stress on relationship and sociality, process thought helps us.

In this chapter I have tried to present a process Christology. Nobody is more aware than I that it needs amplification and explication, far beyond anything possible in these pages. Nor is it the only possible "process way" of doing Christology. There have been other attempts, some of them doubtless more successful than my own. Some process thinkers may feel that this particular attempt is not always consistent with what they regard as essential aspects of that conceptuality; and some Christian theologians may feel dissatisfied on their own account. Therefore I return at the end to what I said at the beginning.

To my mind process thought provides the best available conceptuality for us to use today in the christological enterprise. It is not *the* truth; I doubt if it is possible for us humans to know *the* truth. Yet this conceptuality is highly compatible with biblical emphases, as I have sought to show. For that reason, it may be of help to us as we carry on in our generation the task which faces *all* Christian generations: to say something significant and illuminating about "the message of Christ in all its riches" (Col. 3:16).

10

Church and Ministry in Process Thinking

One of the theological issues to which much attention has been given in recent years is the significance of the Church and with it the related doctrine of ministry. In earlier days, this was not so; perhaps the close identification of the Church with the society in which it had its existence made such consideration seem unnecessary. More likely, however, is the fact that for many years Christian men and women were not self-conscious about their being Christian; theology tends not to concern itself overmuch with what is simply taken for granted. In this instance, the Christian fellowship was accepted gratefully but naturally and easily, while the ministry was part of an established order of things that could also be accepted without much fuss.

Of course there were various views of the meaning of Church and ministry, differing among Christian groups from earlier times, through the Reformation onwards. But it was always assumed that the Church was indeed what St. Paul said it was, "the Body of Christ" and "the household of the faith," with the ordained minister as the person designated to preside in worship, to proclaim the gospel, to administer the sacraments, and to shepherd the flock of Christ. But nowadays, with the sharper perception of the distinction between world and Church—but not the total separation of the two, which surely must be rejected—and with the growing awareness of Christian discipleship as a distinctive reality, theologians of all stripes and persuasions are giving attention to a more formal definition of Church and ministry. And thanks to the growing sense of Christian ecumenicity they are seeking to work out a definition that will be inclusive of the values found in the several traditions which we have inherited and in which we stand.

It is not my intention in this chapter to engage in a discussion of what might be styled formal ecclesiology. I wish only to suggest an approach to understanding the Church and hence of its ministry which will assume as given the New Testament material on the subject, but which will look at this, as well as at the contemporary life of the Christian community from a particular perspective: the conceptuality which is styled process thought. It is my conviction that if we do this, we shall be enabled to see the Church and its ministry in a much more vital and dynamic way than has been common in the past; and furthermore that a good many of the troublesome problems that arise when differing Christian groups discuss their particular attitudes and arrangements will be, not so much solved, as put in a different light and perhaps understood as really less important than they have been thought to be.

First of all, then, I must again say something about process thought itself, although elsewhere in this book I have discussed it at considerable length. When I use that phrase, I am indicating a view of things—of God, the world, and human life—which stresses the living, moving, developing, and changing reality with which we are familiar. The world is no closed and finished affair; it is a process in which within a general continuity there is the appearance of novelty. Human existence was not once created in the distant past and continues forever exactly as it was; it too is developing and moving, marked by a "becoming" which is as real as the "becoming" that characterizes the world in which we live. God is not some absolute, immutable, impassible, self-contained first cause or principle of being; God is the living, active, concerned, and related, yet never exhausted nor confined, reality who is to be adored because he is nothing other than the infinite Love of which Charles Wesley's hymns speak.

The basic constituents of the cosmos are not things but events or happenings: a thing *is* what it *does,* as I have frequently urged in earlier chapters. The energy-events of which the cosmos is composed are no isolable monads but are mutually affected and affective, for ours is a social cosmos, a process marked by sociality and organic in quality. Furthermore, everything in the cosmos is moving toward, or moving away from, the realization of potentialities which are given as possibilities. There is a freedom running through what is not a deterministic mechanism but an open creation, where decisions both "matter and have consequences," as Whitehead said: consequences for which the deciding agents must accept responsibility. In such a world each of us is intended to become human. We are or we are not "on the way" toward that end by our own decisions. These are made all the more difficult, if not nearly impossible, by the inherited accumulation of negative decisions which have rejected possible human fulfillment and settled for less adequate, and hence less satisfactory, ends.

In this context, Christian faith is the affirmation that in the total event we name Jesus Christ the undergirding and circumambient reality we call God is revealed in act, in a fashion so signal and decisive that it makes a difference, a profound and inescapable difference, and invites commitment to him as expressed there in concrete human terms. Yet what is given in that event is not unique in the sense that it is totally alien to what God everywhere is up to; on the contrary, it is the "re-presentation"— to use Schubert Ogden's phrase—or the focal and classical instance, to use my own way of putting it, of the nature of God and his activity everywhere and always. God is Love, John (4:8 and 16) tells us; and since God is always and everywhere Love he always and everywhere acts lovingly in and with his world. To be grasped by this, to respond to this, and to live in terms of this, is to be on the way to true human existence—and the "this" is not our own speculation or theory but the consequence of that which God has "determined, dared, and done" in the Man Jesus.

Now in this process perspective the Christian Church is the community or *social process* which came into existence in response to the total fact of Jesus Christ. It is a community in which the response is made effective and real, since nobody in a social cosmos is "an island entire unto itself." We all live together, we belong together, we are men and women together. And in the fellowship of such people, knit into unity by their common response to the fact of Christ, Christian faith and worship, like Christian discipleship, find their expression. As St. Paul tells us, we are members one of another; and in virtue of our being grasped by the reality of Jesus, historic Master and risen Lord, we are participating in a life which the same Apostle again and again describes as being "in Christ"—*in Christo*. This community is "a new creation," in the sense that it appeared as a result of a new fact, Christ himself; and it has been the means by which that fact has been communicated down through the centuries to men and women in succeeding generations. In that same sense, nobody can be a Christian apart from the Church; every Christian by definition is a "churchman."

Yet just here we need to be on our guard lest we fall into static or mechanical ways of thinking about the community. As I argued in my Colgate-Rochester lectures of a few years ago,[1] the Church *is* "a social process." Because it is that, it is vital, living, dynamic. In Cardinal Newman's sense, as stated in one of his profound moments, it is a *changing* reality, even though it is always given specific identity by its continued and continuing response to the historical fact from which it took its origin.

Every event in the world-process lives from its past, in its present, and toward its future. So with the Church. Its *past* is remembered; and here is the place and point of Scripture, whose basic significance in this context is to tell us "how we got this way." That past becomes available in the *present,* through the proclamation of the Word, which is the bold declaration of the originating event for what it really accomplished, and through the celebration of the sacraments, especially the Eucharist or Lord's Supper in which the past comes alive again in contemporary experience as we "remember" the Lord we follow, just as in another way it comes alive in the proclamation; and similarly through the continued witness in Christian discipleship and Christian action to the personalized principle of life which is "the love of God in Christ Jesus our Lord." And the *future* is also constantly in view, as the Church labors ceaselessly to "prepare and make ready the way" for God to give, or bring in, his Kingdom. Here is the eschatological perspective which is integral to the whole enterprise of Christian existence in community.

This three-fold character tells us that we need always to make sure that we do not minimize any of the tenses: past, present, or future. All three are necessary to the full-orbed reality of the life of the Christian community. To dwell in the past is to reduce Christianity to an archaeological curiosity; to dwell in the present is to fall victim to the cult of contemporaneity; to dwell in the future is to allow oneself the luxury of unrealistic idealism. Each of the three requires the other two; each of them is qualified by the other two. That which the *past* gives us must be prehended in the present, as process thinkers would say; but it must be prehended in a fashion appropriate to our own situation and condition. For example the inherited faith is continually required to experience what Pope John XXIII called *aggiornamento*. It must be "up-dated," which does not mean negated or minimized but rather means that it is to be given expression in a fashion meaningful and relevant to our own day. The *present* adaptation, along with the present ordering of the community's life and its implementation in behavior and action, must be the outgrowth of our past, not something brand-new and "reeking of the spur of the moment," as somebody once phrased it. The *future* is the fulfilled realization of past and present: God's Kingdom, for which we look and for whose coming we prepare, is not the denial of what God has done before now and what he is doing at this moment. God is faithful to his single purpose of love-in-action and the Kingdom or reign of God is nothing other and nothing more than the actualizing, completely and without defect, of that abiding purpose. The reign of God as Love is to be expressed in a world caught up into and in response to himself as precisely that Love.

When we see the Church in this fashion, we can readily understand that the ordained ministry of the community is not to be regarded as a ministry of status but as a ministry of function. In an older day, perhaps, when the world was regarded as made up of fixed and static entities, a conception of ministry as static, and hence a ministry of status, may have been possible. Today this is not the case. Nor would it ever have been entertained, if theologians and others had grasped the functional view of ministry which the New Testament presents to us. Thus the ordained person does not stand apart from and speak "at" the Church; on the contrary, he or she represents and acts for the Church in its wider and more inclusive ministering, on God's behalf, to the world and to its own membership. Such a conception of ministry inevitably demands a rejection of the frequently found conventional notion of complete separation of minister and people; it also demands a rejection of the frequently found notion of a simple identity of minister and congregation. It requires a conception of ministry which sees that in a social process there must be particular agencies with specific responsibilities, in order that the whole process may be enabled to go forward with its work.

Hence an ordained minister is not some separated person who works "upon" others, for their good; neither is that minister simply another "layperson" who for some reason assumes leadership in worship and the proclamation of the gospel. Rather, an ordained minister is "set apart," as we perhaps unhappily phrase it, and hence authorized to stand for the Church's total ministry, which is nothing other than the continuing ministry of Christ in the world. As such the ordained person is to proclaim, to celebrate, and to shepherd, as an enabling agency within and acting for the whole Body of Christ—for what Vatican Council II so rightly styled "the People of God."

This is why there is deep truth in the notion of "succession"— not mere historical succession in the exclusive sense of "episcopal ordination" nor in the conventional repetition of traditional formulae, but succession in the profounder sense of a continuation of the functions of proclamation, celebration, and shepherding, along with witness. The names used to describe this and the method employed to give outward expression to its importance may differ enormously. But if the past is efficacious in the present, and if the present is a decision for the use of the inherited past in ways that are relevant to contemporary existence and future development, then the significance of succession in the sense I have suggested is obvious. We live *from* it, although we cannot live *in* it. A continuing of the same modes of functioning—with the declaration of the fact of Christ, the celebration in the Eucharist of his coming and of the world in which he appears, and the care of God's children who are Christ's brethren—guarantees that in the direction taken and in the development which follows, the community's existence has an identity that makes it exactly itself and not something else. Above all, it gives us a sense of belonging to a living reality whose roots are in the past, whose aim is toward a fulfilled future, but whose present existence is the presentness of the Lord Jesus himself.

In such a perspective we need not be afraid of the attempt to find new ways of stating the abiding Christian gospel, for our

basic allegiance is not to ancient formulae but to the facts of experience, and the experience of facts, to which those formulae
point. Nor need we worry when new modes of worship are
adopted, since it is not the inherited liturgies but the making-
present of Christ in sacramental Eucharistic action which is the
heart of the matter. In respect to the manner of Christian life, with
its moral imperatives, "new occasions teach new duties," with
consequent new ways of understanding Christian witness and expressing Christian concern, since the basic loyalty of the Church
and its members is to the abiding reality of Love-in-act and not to
conventional ideas or codes of moral behavior or human activity,
however ancient and hallowed by centuries of acceptance these
may be.

What I am getting at is a picture of the Christian community as
so much a living enterprise that it answers to the vitalities of human experience. Often enough the "old ways" are good ways and
need only some refurbishing. But time and again, alas, the Christian Church has seemed to be "stuck in the mud" and not able to
move on. The moving-on about which I speak is not an aping of
contemporary fashion; it is the ongoing of God in his world as he
does what Isaiah tells us is characteristic of him: "See, I am doing
a new deed" (43:19). Our confidence is that the new things that
God is doing in the wider world are in accordance with the one
thing that he has done in Christ; in our traditional faith *he* is the
clue or key to our understanding of the divine purpose in creation.
The trouble with static views of Christian community is that they
fail to "keep up with God," not that they are lacking in immediate
appeal. This brings me to my final point.

The Christian Church as a living social process is informed by
the life of the One who lived and died and has been taken into
God's own life; it rests back upon a conviction that the Holy Spirit
is made known in the fellowship as the "Lord and the Life-giver,"
as the Nicene Creed puts it. We have been promised that the Spirit
will lead us "into all truth." But truth is not something static: it is a
doing—"to do the truth" is the Johannine way of speaking about
it. This is the reason for welcoming the charismatic revival in all
parts of Christendom, even though we may feel that some of the
manifestations of that revival seem to be overly emotional and
too subjective. It is also the reason for action towards human
liberation.

"It is the Spirit that gives life"; and one of the reasons for the deadness of so much ecclesiastical business is that the Spirit has been forgotten in an over-zealous concern to maintain the letter. We need a new awareness of the presence and the power of the Spirit in the Church. To my mind, one of the ways toward that new awareness will be through a revision of our conception of the meaning of Church and ministry. I have urged that a process approach will be of great help to us in this task, as in many others. What is more, I believe that the emergence of that conceptuality, with its stress upon activity and event, upon becoming and belonging, upon doing and acting, and above all upon the absolute primacy of Love as our clue to the nature of God, his intention for the world, and the divine purpose for men and women, is one (but of course not the only) indication of the Spirit's working in the affairs of the Church and of the world.

11

Injustice and Liberation

In earlier chapters in this book we have discussed the facts of evil and suffering in a world whose basic thrust and drive, whose supreme reality, we have insisted, is nothing other than sheer Love: *God is Love*, in the phrase from 1 John (4:8) in the New Testament. Our treatment of evil and suffering may have made it clear that the process approach to Christian faith can be of great help to us in considering the wrong, both natural and human, which we experience in a world such as we know. In this chapter I wish to turn briefly to a related topic—and one that is much in the fore these days: the question of the appalling injustice from which so many millions of men and women and children suffer, in all parts of the globe. And with that question must also be related the movements, of various sorts and in different places, toward human liberation.

Certainly one of the major concerns for Christian faith and practice today is just here. If we take with utmost seriousness the conviction that God's "nature and name is Love"; if at the same time we acknowledge, often with anguish, the way in which God's human children have been deprived of elemental rights, treated as slaves, or manipulated to serve the interests of dominant classes or groups—if we do these two things, we are impelled to look honestly at this situation and to understand clearly that we have an inescapable responsibility both to speak and to act for the establishment of a just state of affairs in any and every part of the planet. We cannot evade this by saying that this is not our own immediate concern nor by pretending that in any event we are in no position to work for such genuine freedom as shall bring dignity to all the world's people, enabling them to do more than merely "exist," and opening up for them the possibility of knowing and enjoying abundant life here and now, in this present finite creation.

What if anything can a process theology have to say about all this? I believe that it can speak very positively, even if it does not subscribe to some of the "ideologies" which have been advanced in recent times. Let us set down the main points in which a process approach to this question of injustice and liberation may be expressed.

1. I must first urge that there is no conflict between love and justice in a process theology. Justice is the expression of true love or concern, once we are dealing with humankind in its larger social groupings. If love is to be active, it must find expression in a genuine devotion to the cause of human justice—which is to say that love will be fraudulent if it does not lead to action toward human freedom. And that means that ways must be found by which love may work in that direction.

Some have spoken as if love were primarily, if not solely, a matter of one-to-one personal relationships: "I" and "Thou," to use Buber's well-known mode of statement. But this will not do, since the greater part of our human existence is in terms of "I" and "*you*"—it has to do with more than this or that other single individual. We have stressed the process insight that to be human *is* to be a social creature. All of us live with, as we depend upon, our brothers and sisters; and without that social "belonging" we are not human at all. What is more, to pretend to some individual self-sufficiency is to fight against the very grain of the universe, in which anything and everything influences and affects anything and everything else.

Not only does the process conceptuality see things in this fashion, however. The Christian faith itself speaks of our being "parts of one body" (1 Cor. 12:27); it insists that if any one part hurts *all* parts hurt with it and that each part should be concerned for all the others. When one human being is underprivileged, denied his or her proper human rights, or treated without dignity and without respect, every other human being is diminished. Eugene V. Debs, the famous American socialist leader of the earlier years of this century, said that so long as there is *one* person unjustly in prison, *all the rest of us* are in the same situation. Class, race, social or educational background, and whatever other factors may be involved cannot for the Christian be a matter of indifference; we are, as I have quoted earlier from John Donne, "part of the main" and none of us dare deem ourselves "an island entire unto itself." To talk and to act in that fashion is to blaspheme: it is to deny in practice that the love of God is indeed reflected in and part of the reality of love of the neighbor. Hence Christians must concern themselves with these deeply social implications of the faith which in worship and in other ways is affirmed.

2. On the other hand, if love leads to justice, it is also true that justice without love can be cold, indifferent, and without the warmth and human quality which Christian faith entails. To work for human rights in that chilly manner is to be less than concerned with men and women as children of God's love and therefore as persons to be loved by all who profess to trust in him. I suspect that one reason that many people in situations of rank injustice dislike what used to be called "the liberals' " interest in their welfare is precisely here. Nobody wants to be the recipient of "charity," in the pejorative sense of that word. There is a story about a Cockney woman who was often visited by a noble lady who condescended to "help her." The Cockney woman finally got irritated at this treatment and said, "I wish that you'd stop coming here to 'save your soul' on me." Exactly so: nothing can be so dehumanizing as that sort of conduct. "The gift without the giver is bare," the old proverb tells us. The point here is that the mere "doing of justice," the loveless effort to achieve human rights for all men and women, and similar activity for "the good" of others, can often seem to the victims of such interest as nothing less than humiliating.

Hence, both from the stance of Christian faith and also from the position taken in respect to human relationships in a process perspective, mutuality or sharing, which are the expression of genuine love in its deepest sense, are requisite. What is more, that sort of love for others provides both the motive for and the manifestation of a real, not a pretended, devotion to the men and women who are known to be deprived of the opportunity for proper expression of their human potentialities.

3. There is no specific guidance, either from the process side or from Christian faith, as to the particular political programs or

detailed measures which should be adopted in order to secure human rights and bring about human liberation from bondage. Here some of us are obliged to part company from others of us who share a profound devotion to the battle for human dignity and freedom but demand specific action as a lone Christian. Whatever else may be thought about remarks made by Pope John Paul II at Puebla, not long ago, and on other occasions too, surely there can be no doubt that he was speaking both wisely and Christianly when he urged that the motive for participating in this struggle, and also the ways in which that participation is implemented, cannot for a Christian be what he styled "godless Marxism" in its programmatic form and in its basic philosophical stance. On the other hand, those of us who dissent from such programs and such theoretical grounds may very well discover that cooperation with those who do hold these to be valid is an essential aspect of our struggle. On the one hand, we dare not refuse such cooperation because others with whom we disagree take to it a different approach from our own; on the other hand, such practical cooperation need not, and for some of us cannot, entail a confusion of motive and concrete ways of acting. A Christian can act only from love and for love; process thinkers can work only in consequence of their belief that the cosmos as a whole is on the side of goodness and righteousness and that to fail to engage in a struggle for the freedom of others is to attempt to fight against the basic dynamic of the cosmos.

4. What about so-called liberation theology? Some of us believe that this is a misnomer. There is no "liberation theology," any more than there is a "black theology" or a "feminist theology" or a "gay theology." There is only *theology*, which is the attempt to formulate and state, in as consistent and coherent a fashion as can be humanly attained, the relationship between God and the creation, with the many corollaries which a sound understanding of that relationship will suggest or demand. "Feminist theology" ought to be theology done with a sincere and glad acceptance of what the female experience may have to tell the rest of us. "Black theology" ought to be theology which takes very seriously the experience of men and women who have undergone the tragic deprivations and rejection which have been so dreadfully imposed upon persons and groups of black color and racial

inheritance. "Gay theology" is theology which takes account of
the orientation and attitudes of men and women who are homo-
sexually inclined. And "liberation theology" ought not to be
something quite distinct and different from other theology; but
rather to be theology which is keenly aware of, deeply concerned
about, and genuinely involved in stating the reasons for the free-
ing of vast numbers of God's children from the injustice and
bondage which has been so terribly a part of their human experience.

The position which has just been stated will doubtless be rejected by many significant thinkers, writers, and activists. Nonetheless, regard for the total integrity of the theological discipline
seems to make this position necessary. Nor is there the slightest
reason to think that this position will diminish the intensity of the
concern for the human struggle and hence will fail to recognize
and insist that no Christian can refuse to take part in that struggle.
Furthermore, those of us who adopt this position can learn much
from, and therefore be greatly indebted to, the defenders of a
quite different way of seeing things.

5. This is not the place, nor have we here the necessity, for spell-
ing out in more detail exactly what might be appropriate proce-
dures for the development of this struggle. It will suffice to say
that any convinced Christian, who has understood the implications of the faith, cannot refuse to play his or her part in that
movement. There may be, doubtless there will be, "diversities of
operation"—depending upon opportunities offered, possibilities
for meaningful support, and ways of positive and practical activity. But there will be "one and the self-same Spirit," the Spirit
which is nothing other than God's working in the hearts and
through the deeds of his human children to bring all of them to
that freedom, that dignity, and that self-esteem, which will open
for them the chance of true and abundant living here and now.

In Latin America, in Africa, in Asia—yes, and in North
America and Europe too—the dependable, worshipful, and supreme Lover of the world whom we call "our God" is at work,
often in very secular fashion, to bring about a society in which
there is justice for all. To be a fellow-worker with that cosmic
Lover is to respond to the call and lure which makes us discontented with our own ease and comfort; it is to be, with God, what

Whitehead styled a "co-creator" of a greater and more widely shared social good. The Christian imperative thus to labor, combined with the process insight into the basic dynamic and structure of reality, is inescapable. Failure to play one's part in that movement is to be nothing other than an "unprofitable servant." This is why and how Christian process theology can serve as a context and motivation for the fullest support of any and every effort to liberate men and women and children from servitude to economic, political, and social systems that deny them the dignity which is both their proper nature and their intended destiny.

6. In still another way, process thought is significant in this connection. As I have urged in earlier chapters, the affirmation of process thinkers is that the world in which we live and of which we are a part is one that has as its basic characteristic change, development, or "process." Any static view of the world is rejected as untrue to the facts which we now know. Such an understanding rules out completely the notion, often so popular in conventional religious circles, that we have to do with a rigid world-order in which nothing genuinely new can make its appearance. On the contrary, we are confronted by, and we also have our place in, a created order that is open to novelty: in the words of an earlier philosopher, "There is continuity of process with the emergence of genuine novelty." If that is the case, then we shall expect that change, for better or for worse, will take place; and we shall also know that we are called to be agents of that charge.

The biblical interpretation of the creation follows along the same lines. God says to the prophet Isaiah, "See I am doing *new* deeds" (Isa. 43:19), and in the book of Revelation we read, "Now I am making the whole of creation new" (Rev. 21:5). In other words, the main drive of the scriptural witness is not to stress a static and entirely completed creation but to emphasize the way in which, in response to the divine lure, there is a freshness about things. Hence we can *expect* that there will be novelty; everything is not "fixed."

In such a perspective, movements like that for human liberation find their place. When such movements make their appearance, as in our own day, we can rightly say that they are part of the divine activity in its unceasing operation in human affairs. In them there is a divine initiative, to which men and women may (or may not) make their proper response. And the divine call is for a positive response, in which humankind will open itself to be both a reflection of, and instrumental for, the divine purpose of more good—and that includes true justice and the liberation of God's children from oppression—in more places, at more times, in more ways, and for more people.

This should not lead us to think that there is some inevitable progression toward the better in a world such as we inhabit. On the contrary, every opportunity for good is accompanied by the temptation to reject that possibility, while (as the old saying has it) "the higher we may rise, the farther we may fall." Human self-centeredness, pride, desire for control, and the like are always present with us and in us. The doctrine of "original sin," whatever may be its defects, ought to make that plain enough to any thoughtful and observant person. A former colleague of mine once remarked, "The story of the human race is all about our discovering more subtle ways of 'sinning.' " I accepted this; but I added, "And the Christian faith is that *God's* story is all about his finding more subtle ways of dealing with that 'sinning.' "

It is for this reason that we are challenged, although we may not be compelled, to respond wholeheartedly to the struggle for human liberation and to fight with our sisters and brothers against any and every form of injustice and oppression. A very great deal depends, then, on human cooperation. God wills to act through our free assent as his agents.

7. In one of his books, Whitehead said that the aim or intention basic to the world is to make it possible for the creatures "to live, to live well, and to live better."[1] This is "the art of life," he affirmed; and he argued that "reason is a factor in experience which directs and criticizes the urge towards the attainment of an end realized in imagination but not in fact"; while he saw also that human effort is directed toward realizing this end *in fact*, so far as our finite situation and human capability makes this possible.

Now there are two ways in which a world view may be seen. One is to regard it as merely a theoretical account of how things are and of how they go. The other is more practical. Indeed, Karl Marx once said that whereas in the past philosophy has been concerned with the former and more theoretical aspect, now it must strive to "change the world." Whitehead would have agreed at this point. A process perspective is not only a helpful interpretation of the state of affairs; it is also, and even more importantly, a position which makes the effort for change both desirable and imperative.

No advocate of Christian process theology can be a spectator only; if he or she seeks to be this, it will be in disloyalty to the deepest thrust of the conceptuality that has been accepted. And for the ordinary Christian believer, there is an equal demand that he or she shall put convictions to work in concrete action—and in our day that means work for human freedom and dignity.

8. But both Christian faith and the process way of seeing the world and human life make the easy use of violence undesireable. If process theology's development of Christian faith into a coherent and systematic reality is anywhere near the truth, it will be ready to affirm that the use of violence is ultimately counterproductive. Why is this? Because deep down in the world, basic to its dynamic and structure, is not sheer coercion or force, but genuine persuasion or love. It may appear otherwise, to be sure; it takes "a lot of looking and a lot of believing," as a friend has put it, to affirm, and then to act upon, the affirmation that in the long run the only way to achieve a just society is through persuasive means. For some of us, this leads to the conviction that violent revolutionary methods are bound to be self-defeating. Perhaps we may claim, with considerable factual evidence to support us, that this is demonstrably the case.

To say that, however, does not rule out for us other kinds of pressure, through demonstrations, through "passive resistance" (as with Gandhi in India), through insistent argument, through brave witness to justice, through forceful rejection of any and all ways in which men and women are denied their human rights. It may even be necessary to overthrow, by as peaceful a means as possible, tyrannical and despotic regimes. But the adoption of violence or bloody revolution as the proper way to secure what we see is needed seems to some of us a fatal descent to a less than truly human, hence a less than properly divine, mode of behavior. Patience is required; and sometimes patience is not easy when we feel outrage at the indecent treatment of others. Yet if history teaches us anything, it is the truth of the old Latin adage, *festina lente*: "to make haste slowly" is usually the most certain way in which the right ends will be achieved.

9. Finally, process theology believes that it is *in God*, and in God alone, that all true good, like all beauty and righteousness and truth, will find reception and further employment. Christian hope has often been misconceived; it has been put not in God but in what we think that God will give us, if only we are "nice." In another book, called *After Death: Life in God,*[2] I have argued the point; I shall not repeat it here. But this much must be said. All our efforts to secure justice, all our labor for human liberation, and all that these efforts and that labor may achieve, are *surely safe in God.* The divine reality who is the primal creative agency is also the final receptive reality. God treasures the good that is done in the world; he can and does use it for further implementation of good, as he continues the ceaseless divine striving to bring out of the sometimes almost intractable material of a created order, a harmony in which significant and necessary contrast need not bring about senseless and destructive conflict. To work with God toward that end, here and now in this mortal life, is or ought to be both a challenge and a reward. To serve toward that end, and not to ask for any recompense "save the knowledge that we do God's will" (as St. Ignatius Loyola phrased it), is enough for any truly dedicated Christian disciple.

12

Epilogue: Whitehead and Catholicism

In his autobiography *Memories and Meanings,*[1] Dr. W. R. Matthews, one-time Dean of St. Paul's Cathedral in London, wrote briefly about his friendship with Alfred North Whitehead. They had both been associated with the University of London, where Matthews was Dean of King's College and Whitehead a professor at the Imperial College of Science and Technology. Their friendship continued after Matthews went to St. Paul's and Whitehead to Harvard University in the United States. Matthews was the guest of the Whiteheads when he visited Harvard to give lectures, and their relationship was always warm and affectionate despite the miles which separated them.

His notes about Whitehead show the deep sympathy and appreciation of the Dean for his old friend. Brief as they are, his remarks provide an interesting insight into some aspects of Whitehead's life and belief which have not received very much attention and which deserve to be more generally understood.

For our present concern, one paragraph in Matthews' account is of special interest. The Dean tells us that one day Whitehead said to him, "The older I get, the more certain I am that nearly all the things Catholics do are right, and nearly all the reasons they give are wrong." The Dean couples this with the comment that in his view "specimens of his [Whitehead's] conversation which are on record are defective." Presumably he is referring to the material which Lucien Price included in his *Dialogues of Alfred North Whitehead*,[2] published shortly after the latter's death and still available. The "specimens" are "defective," Matthews goes on to say, because "they do not convey the religious spirit of Whitehead's thinking." Further, Matthews says that while "sharply critical comments on the apparent contradictions and confusions in Christian teaching are authentic and characteristic," it is equally true that Whitehead "spoke from within the fellowship of the spiritually awakened. He was a worshipper."

These words of Dean Matthews seem to me to be of very considerable interest; they deserve our closest attention since they indicate a side of Whitehead that should receive much more notice than it has done. What is more, they show that the use of Whitehead's thought by process theologians is not an accidental matter but has its basis in the deeply religious spirit and concern of the man himself.

Not only did Matthews know Whitehead well. He also had a considerable appreciation of his friend's philosophical views, although he quite correctly notes that such a book as *Process and Reality* is "written in a most difficult idiom which the reader has to acquire before he can understand the work." That certainly is true enough; but unfortunately Matthews also expresses some doubt as to whether "Whitehead's influence will be lasting." The Dean was writing in his old age, for he was almost ninety when his autobiography appeared; he was evidently not aware of the growing influence of Whitehead's process thought in recent years, not only in the United States but to some degree in Britain and significantly in Latin countries. Nor does he seem to know about the development of that conceptuality by Christian theologians as a way of engaging in the reconstruction of doctrine. But it is precisely the fact of that development which makes Matthews' earlier remarks so valuable, for they bring into focus an aspect of the man and his thought which has not received proper attention from many Whitehead scholars.

My concern in this chapter is with that aspect; and more particularly with it as it has to do with "the things Catholics do" and "the reasons they give." When this is linked with what Matthews tells us about "the religious spirit of Whitehead's teaching," I believe that we are compelled to reckon very seriously with that "religious spirit" and with the fact that Whitehead was indeed sympathetic with what we may style the "Catholic" side of the broad Christian tradition, whatever may have been his disagreement with much of its theology and with the metaphysical assumptions upon which that theology so frequently rests. I shall endeavor in this chapter to consider this subject, not least because in this book I have been especially concerned with a reconception of Christian doctrine following the line taken by Whitehead himself in his later writings.

1. I was myself first brought to realize this sympathy with "Catholic Christianity"—I put this in inverted commas because I mean here not only the Roman Catholic Church but also Anglo-Catholicism in the Church of England and the wider Anglican Communion, in which I was brought up in my youth—when I was told that during his days in the English Cambridge, where he lived and worked for some thirty years, Whitehead had attended worship with I do not know what regularity at what would be called a "high church" parish. He had also attended services in the chapel of Trinity, his own college, and liked to be present from time to time at the afternoon service (even then celebrated for the splendor of its music) at the chapel of my own college, King's. A former student of Whitehead's at Harvard had informed me that after his arrival in the American Cambridge, Whitehead took to attending now and again the worship of one of the "high church" parishes in Boston, although later he discontinued this practice and only went occasionally to the services in the Memorial Chapel of Harvard University.

One of my students pointed out to me what I had not myself noticed, that the only reference in *Process and Reality* to a specifically religious symbol has to do with incense.[3] Whitehead recognized the dangerous side of such a symbol, yet he said that "for many purposes, certain aesthetic experiences which are easy to produce make better symbols than do words, written or spoken." "Incense is a suitable symbol," he said, for producing "certain religious emotions"; at the same time he was sure that there must be a real communication of the meaning to be conveyed, and the emotions produced must be sound and genuine. The specific instance of incense is probably of no great importance; what matters is that Whitehead *used* that instance and thus made obvious his appreciation of its place in Catholic worship. Another former student of his at Harvard reported to me that Whitehead had once, in his hearing, defended "Catholic modes of worship" but had spoken critically of what he styled the "literalistic" and "rationalistic" teaching often associated with them. This is not unlike his comment to Matthews which was quoted at the beginning of this chapter.

Price in the *Dialogues* reports Whitehead's favorable comment on a Mass which he had attended in a German cathedral. Here, he said, "was an immense concourse of devout people; you couldn't hear a thing that was being said, and it was perfect. You had a sense that the religious office was going on, and you shared it with all those pious people."[4] He went on to say that he had also been profoundly moved by a Quaker service, in its utter simplicity; and the connection of the two, Catholic and Quaker, was an indication of his sense that worship at its best is not a lecture or ethical exhortation but something much more profound. Reading this made me think of von Hügel's insistence that there is a similarity between such Catholic worhip and Quaker silence: in each of them the "sacred" is felt and adored and *words* do not matter so much. Still a third student of Whitehead's reported to me that his teacher had once remarked on the aesthetic appeal of Catholic worship; he believed that the aesthetic has its deep religious significance, but he admitted that he himself could not consider his philosophy reconcilable with "orthodox Christianity" although he still could think of himself as a Christian. Here of course everything depends on what is meant by "orthodoxy"; it is evident that for Whitehead this meant the doctrinal position his own father (a priest of the Church of England) held and also the theological formulations in Western Christianity with which he was so unhappy.

I need not cite the many references to Christian faith and theology found particularly in *Adventures of Ideas* and *Religion in the Making*, and in one essay in *Science and the Modern World*.[5] From all these it is apparent that Whitehead understood religion as a cultural phenomenon but that he also believed firmly that the "religious vision," and more particularly what he styled "the brief Galilean vision," were important as clues to *the way things go* in the creative advance. Of course this material, and much else in his writings, has to be sorted out. What *was* his religious position? How are we to understand it and him? Such questions may lead us to a renewed study of his thought, especially if we are (like myself) in one way or another "disciples" of this master of philosophy.

Until Professor Victor Lowe publishes the biography upon which he has been working for many years, we shall not have all the data we might wish. Yet I believe that while we cannot work out fully the story of Whitehead's religious beliefs and their development over the years, or at least cannot do this with any precision, we can certainly see how he began and we can have a pretty good idea of where he ended. In this connexion, of course, we must be on our guard against taking *au pied de la lettre* some of the comments reported by Lucien Price. The sharp criticism of certain Old Testament material, to mention but one instance, or the fact that he said that during the war years he found the Bible to be of little help to him, to take another instance, may very well be true. Price states that Whitehead said just this. But we need to remember that such comments, like many others, are *obiter dicta* of a man in his eighties. They should not be used to undermine or deny his considered opinions expressed in his books, which (as we know also from Price) were carefully worked out and carefully phrased. The *obiter dicta* are to be seen in the light of his considered views, not *vice versa*.

I believe that we may think with some confidence that Whitehead held to the central Christian insight throughout his life—save perhaps for a very short period, when (according to Bertrand Russell's recollection) he was "agnostic." At the same time, we must grant that he was impatient with traditional formulae for expressing that insight and was saddened, if not angered, by the errors which, in his judgment, had been brought about in the ongoing Christian tradition by "alien ideas" imported from moralistic notions, substantialist metaphysics, and a rigid dogmatic stance, as well as from the imperial cult of the Roman and Byzantine empires.

2. First, then, how did Whitehead *begin*?

His background was entirely Christian, not to say clerical. His father was a clergyman of the Church of England, vicar of St. Peter's in Ramsgate on the Isle of Thanet in Kent. He was a conservative parson of "the old school," particularly fond of the Old Testament, whose texts he "thundered" (as Whitehead put it) under the high vaulting of his ancient church. Whitehead's brother became a clergyman and eventually was made a missionary bishop of the Church of England in India. As a child, Whitehead imbibed Christian teaching at home, attended services in his father's church, and knew ecclesiastical dignitaries like the great Archbishop Tait, his father's close friend, who was accustomed to drive frequently from Canterbury to visit the Ramsgate vicarage. Later, when at school in the ancient foundation of Sherborne in Dorset, he received regular religious instruction, was confirmed in his "teens," and was enormously impressed by the tradition of which that school, which a few years ago celebrated its thousandth anniversary, was a living part. He became interested in Christian missions and made an annual contribution to the Church Missionary Society during his early years as an undergraduate and later a junior fellow at Cambridge.

Either as a junior fellow, or more likely later as a senior fellow and lecturer, he had a brief period of "agnosticism," if Bertrand Russell's memory is to be trusted. But we have no further details of this; and Russell himself tells us that at one point his teacher, who was later his friend and colleague, was thinking seriously of conversion to the Roman Catholic Church. This was because of his meeting with, and reading the books of, Cardinal Newman, whom he greatly admired. I have already spoken of his attendance at college chapel and of his going to Little St. Mary's, the "high church" parish next door to Peterhouse in Cambridge. He himself mentioned his attending church with his wife, after he had married Evelyn Wade, of an Irish family but educated in French convents. He also read a great deal of theology, more particularly the works of the "Fathers," the early Christian theologians. This reading is reflected in many of his remarks in one chapter of *Adventures of Ideas*, where he spoke in the highest terms of the valuable contribution of those "Fathers" toward a deepening of the doctrine of God by their insistence on a genuine and direct divine immanence in the world. He told Lucien Price that when he wished to make more room in his library, he sold his theological books; he had read them and there was no reason to retain them on his shelves. We learn from Russell that the death of his son,

Eric, killed in military action in World War I, had a profound effect upon him, having much to do (thinks Russell) with his philosophical development and above all his religious concern.

There can be little doubt, then, that throughout those years, with whatever doubts and granted the brief period of "agnosticism" to which Bertrand Russell refers, Whitehead was essentially a Christian. His beliefs, as he worked them out, may not have been conventional; with much of the theological structure he had learned in childhood he was evidently discontented. The same remained true as the years passed. Over and over again we find in his writings allusions to or discussions of religious and theological questions. In his books, quite as much as in the conversations Price records, he could and did speak scathingly of "official theology"; he could and did denounce parts of the Bible, more particularly in the Old Testament and in the Book of Revelation, which seemed to him either sub-Christian or barbaric and hence unworthy of assent. He could even say, as we have noted, that the Bible helped him much less in his old age than it had done when he was younger, although even then he described it as a great "saga." At the same time he could speak sympathetically and warmly of the spirit of worship and especially of "Catholic worship." He contrasted that worship with the didactic and moralistic type that failed in emphasis on the symbolic with its "holiness of beauty" (as we might phrase it). He disliked the sort of religious exercise which laid its stress on intellectual attitudes or was concerned primarily with moral teaching.

He once mentioned his affection for the English Book of Common Prayer, with its evocation of reverence and beauty. But he criticized Anglicanism, the religion in which he had been brought up, because with all its advantages—the Prayer Book itself, the glory of its cathedrals, the historical splendor of its parish churches—it had (he said) "everything except religion." This is a hard saying, perhaps; but those of us who are Anglicans can understand what he meant. The arid "establishment type" of Anglicanism is indeed often more a cultural than a profoundly religious reality. Yet when true to itself, it (like Roman Catholicism) is available, many of us can say, for genuine worship.

As he grew older he continued to express his deep appreciation of genuine religious insight and faith, but he became ever more impatient with the conventional theological structure which, to his mind, contradicted the deepest intention of that insight and faith. Yet he was equally if not more critical of the kind of liberalism which consisted mainly, in his view, of finding "vapid reasons" for "continuing to go to church in the old way." He felt that liberalism of this sort tended to substitute ethical teaching for genuine religious insight; it was altogether too ready to give up the very notion of "dogma"—which for him meant the ordered statement of the generalizations implicitly contained in the religious vision—in its effort to accommodate itself to the passing fads of the moment. His reverence for Jesus continued and increased; this is obvious from everything that he wrote and said. In the event of Christ there was what he called "the disclosure of the nature of God and his agency in the world." It troubled him that the conventional presentations of the doctrine of God had forgotten, far too often, that remarkable disclosure which had been glimpsed by Plato and others but which had been enacted in the life of Jesus of Nazareth. For that disclosure there had been substituted models of an "Oriental despot," or some "abstract concept" of being or substance, or (perhaps worst of all) a "ruthless moralist." His central concern was with the "brief Galilean vision" where the divine was revealed, through an event of remarkable "importance," as loving and persuasive rather than as coercive and sheerly omnipotent. It was for Christians, he said, "to work out the doctrine" which followed from this fact—here it differed from Buddhism, which began with a doctrine or a metaphysic and then sought for facts to illustrate it.

In his last words, if Price's report is to be trusted, he spoke of the human vocation to be a "co-creator with God," which constituted our dignity and for Whitehead gave life its purpose, whatever might be thought about the possibility of individual survival, consciously speaking, after human death. With this affirmation, expressed in the noble words found on the last pages of the *Dialogues*, Whitehead *ended*. Perhaps we may say that his beginning and his ending were different only in that at the end he spoke with the authority of one who has thought deeply, experienced much, and become as wise as any man of his age and time.

3. With all this in mind, we cannot doubt the accuracy of Dean Matthews' judgment that his friend had a "religious spirit," that

he spoke "from within the fellowship of the spiritually awakened," and that he was most certainly "a worshipper."

That word, "worshipper," is a clue to Whitehead's approach to
religion. Alix Parmentier, the French philosopher who has written a massive study entitled *La philosophie de Whitehead et la
Problème de Dieu* (now being translated into English and likely to
appear in a year or two), is quite correct when she says that for
Whitehead religion was essentially to be found in what she calls
adoration, which is her translation of the English word "worship" so frequently employed by Whitehead. She is also right in
urging that for him love (*l'amour*) was central in his thought
about God. Parmentier is in error, however, when she says that
"creativity" and "love" were in conflict in his thought and that
finally the former concept was given precedence. Her mistake
arises from her failure to see that it was Whitehead's conviction
that a world "in process," interrelated and social in nature, has
creativity as the characteristic of all entities or occasions, including God, serving in this respect much the same purpose that "being" serves in Aristotelian and Thomistic thought. Furthermore,
she does not discern that love was for him the nature or quality of
reality, operative throughout the creative advance, inviting and
evoking the movement toward fulfillment or satisfaction of aim.
There was in fact no conflict nor contradiction between "creativity" and "love." Parmentier is also wrong when she says flatly
that Whitehead rejected a "personal" God. She does not observe
that in speaking of the divine he mentioned what are in fact the
chief characteristics of "personality"—conscious awareness,
freedom, purpose or intention, communication, and relationship. Whitehead was certainly hesitant about the free use of the
words "person" or "personal"; the reason for this, I think, is that
to him the words suggested, or were often taken to mean, limiting
and unhappily anthropomorphic notions and neglected the place
of impersonal "structures" in divine reality, as well as what he
called "the secular functions" of deity.

Worship (*adoration*) was indeed for Whitehead the chief religious activity and expression. He coupled with this a sense of
what he called "companionship" and "refreshment," along with
the "saving" of what had been accomplished in the world so that
this accomplishment might forever be treasured in the divine ex-

perience. For him this position required a "new reformation" in which there would be a reconception of Christian theology, more particularly in order to bring out both the character of God as love or persuasion and also the intimate relationship of God to a world which influences him and has its effects upon him. This meant a rejection of the conventional teaching that in no way does the world provide anything for God, since God is already entirely "self-contained" and in no sense "depends" upon what happens in the creation. If that should be the case, then the creation would be irrelevant to God. He regarded what he was prepared to style "the great apostasy" of traditional Christian thought as the substitution of an "idolatrous conception" of God as absolute power, unaffected substance or being, unmoved mover, "imperial Caesar," and harsh unrelenting moralist. Anything which reflected that substitution was to be subjected to the most severe criticism. In theology, as in liturgy and in patterns of behavior, the false conception had worked devastatingly to alter the content of the "Galilean vision," rendering it either meaningless or irrelevant. Thus he denounced a theology which in "paying metaphysical compliments" to God was prepared to forget the tenderness, gentleness, patience, suffering, justice, and love disclosed in that vision as being nothing less than *the truth* about the divine reality whom men and women worship. Love like this had about it a note of utter triumph and sheer victory, even when it participates (as participate love must) in the world's anguish and suffering. Here is a "tragic view" of the world; here also is an insistence upon the divine sharing in that world's tragedy.

One or two examples may be given, to illustrate what such a reconception demanded. A transactional doctrine of the atonement was for Whitehead a denial of the vision of Love as suffering with men and women, through communion with them saving what is salvable, providing an insight into the way things "go in the world," making possible a right adjustment and a genuine fellowship, and giving his children the dignity of being "cocreators" with God—their contribution accepted by and used in God in further implementation of his abiding purpose of good. Again, Whitehead rejected a view of worship which regarded it as an "endless serenading" of a God supposed to delight in having his creatures cringe in his presence and abase themselves in such a fashion that their proper personhood would be denied. For him, that was not genuine worship; it was more appropriate to the court of a tyrannical despot than to the relationship of human beings to the God whose love enables them to think of him as "Father." Nor did he have any use for the sort of prayer which Dean W. R. Inge once caustically called "pestering the deity with our petitions," as if God could be coerced by this exercise to grant what his children thought they wanted. He remarked that in primitive religions God was invoked to provide for our own wishes, such as they were, while in a developed religion, such as Christianity was supposed to be, God was addressed by his children so that they might be conformed to his likeness and character. Likewise he rejected the kind of piety which regards the creatures as puppets to be manipulated by an entirely omnipotent deity; such a notion seemed to him morally unworthy and a contradiction of the vision of God as persuasive. It also denied the freedom which belongs to any and every entity to realize, within due limits, its own subjective aim in full responsibility for the decisions which that entity may make.

When Whitehead, in his conversations, commended American theistic Unitarianism, as Price reports, it was for its insistence on just that vision of God as Love and just that concern for human freedom and dignity and justice, despite its arid and moralistic way of worship. Thus what has been said, to this point helps us to understand what Whitehead meant when he told Dr. Matthews that what Catholics "do" is, for the most part, right while the reasons they tend to give for doing it are "nearly all wrong."

Let us note that Whitehead commended what "Catholics *do*." We can see what his meaning was, without falling into the trap of setting "denominational Catholics" against "denominational Protestants." Presumably Whitehead was thinking of the way in which, for Catholic Christianity, worship is central and all-important. He was also thinking, I believe—and his occasional comments show this—of the practice of personal confession to a priest acting as God's agent, as a way of relieving the tensions and blockage which so often prevent proper human development as a "lover in the making." With all this, he associated the rich symbolism, the appeal to the senses as well as to the mind and will, and the aesthetic quality in liturgical action such as he had so much appreciated in the German cathedral Mass. For him these would have been related to the stress laid in his general world view on deep "feeling tones" in human experience and the need for what he once styled "purification in the inward parts." We can assume, therefore, that what was in his mind was the broad Catholic sacramental worship and practice which could speak to the whole person, including human rationality and volition, yet at the same time meeting the need, so deep in human experience, for an imaginative response to the divine lure. This also helps us to see why he was attracted to the beauty and solemnity of the Anglican Prayer Book, to the service in the German cathedral, and to the value (even) of incense as a religious symbol.

4. In this way, then, Whitehead was by way of saying to Matthews that the kind of religion or adoration found in "Catholic Christianity" was along the right lines. Such worship fitted in with and gave sense to the wider philosophical stance which he had adopted. Yet the *reasons* which were often given for what Catholic Christianity "does" were, he thought, "nearly all wrong." What did he mean by this comment? I take it that he was implicitly criticizing theological formulations which seemed to him both alien to the essential Christian *ethos* (expressed vividly in "the Galilean vision") and also in themselves open to the gravest suspicion metaphysically and morally.

Professor A. H. Johnson, one-time research student at Harvard under Whitehead, has in his *Whitehead's Philosophy of Civilization*[6] devoted a whole chapter to his teacher's religious ideas and beliefs. That chapter seems to me the most adequate of all discussions I have read on the subject. He says that the view of God held by Whitehead was nothing other than a "generalizing" of what is to be seen in Jesus of Nazareth. I believe that this is correct; for the meaning here is that in Jesus God was disclosed as "Love-in-action." God is revealed "in act"—God is, so to say, "enacted" in that instance of human existence—for what he really is and in what he really does. Insofar as conventional "orthodoxy," of whatever variety, holds to positions which deny or reduce that affirmation, derived as it is from the Galilean disclosure, it is "wrong." It does not give attention to, nor does it make sense of, the focal event in the Christian tradition. It does not fit with the basic criterion provided in that focal event. Love, and

Love only, is the creative dynamic in terms of which any and every religious and theological statement must be evaluated. Any "reason" given for what Catholics "do," any theological formulation of the significance of worship, any interpretation of practice or behavior, must be consonant with that criterion. Otherwise, the formulation will be "wrong."

To say what has just been said indicates that the religious strain in Whitehead's thought, his theistic stress, is integral to his whole metaphysical position, as it is central to an understanding of his attitude toward the significance of human life and experience. It is necessary to say this at this time, when the general Whitehead "vision of reality" is being taken seriously by many philosophers who have been delivered from the sterile negations of a purely linguistic philosophy. But there is a danger that the more general conceptuality will be valued and even accepted but that the specifically religious element, based on Whitehead's own religious vision, will be regarded as merely incidental—a cultural accident, so to say, that is not essential to the system as a whole. Yet without that religious element, and certainly without the theistic stress, Whitehead's metaphysical position is misinterpreted and misunderstood. Theoretically it might be possible to construct a "process metaphysic," largely along Whiteheadian lines, which would not require a concept of deity; but this would not be *Whitehead's* metaphysic but another one. Despite the argument of Donald Sherburne, in his essay "Whitehead without God,"[7] God is no mere addendum to his metaphysic. As "the fellow-suffer who understands," God is inescapably part of the total picture. He is the necessary reason for novelty in the creative advance, through his supplying of new "initial aims"; he is the "chief exemplification" of the principles required to make sense of the world and not an unnecessary feature stuck on as a pious addition but with no indispensable function; he is the lure in and behind all "prehensions"; he is the ultimate recipient of the achievements in creation as well as the *chief* (but rightly, for Whitehead and I should say for any sound theology, not the *only*) causative agency. To drop God from Whitehead's metaphysical vision is to fail in respect for the integrity of that vision—which was all that Whitehead claimed his metaphysic to be. It would be to substitute another vision for Whitehead's own.

This God, integral to the Whiteheadian metaphysic and validated in human religious experience, is then nothing other than Love—I think Whitehead would have been willing to say, a Lover—disclosed vividly in act in the event of Jesus Christ, just as he has elsewhere been "divined in theory" in the thinking of Plato and others, including (as we might now add) the religious prophets and seers and sages of many different cultures and faiths. What is more, God is conceived by Whitehead as supremely "available" for men and women in their religious requirements. He is both "the desire of all nations" and the fulfillment of human yearning. I do not need to repeat here the answers made by Victor Lowe, Charles Hartshorne, and Bernard Loomer to Stephen Ely's claim, made many years ago, that Whitehead's concept of God is *not* thus available. These responses should be read by all who are concerned with this basic question; they may be found in various old issues of *The Journal of Religion, The Review of Religion,* and *Ethics,* during the 1940s. But it may be useful to offer some comments on related matters.

The first comment has to do with Whitehead's recognition, worked out in *Religion in the Making,*[7] that the history of religious advance is through the moralization and rationalization of an original sense of "the sacred." Worship in an immoral or unmoral context is false; so also is worship which is irrational, in that it fails to relate itself to a reasonable account of human experience and the world. But this is not to suggest that worship, as a response to "the sacred," is to be regarded as only a passing phase in human history. Nor does it imply that religion is exhaustively contained in moral imperatives and in the intelligibility of rational concepts. We have already spoken of "adoration"; von Hügel once said that adoration is the very heart of true religion and Whitehead quite obviously agreed with him. The requirement in worship, for Whitehead, is that "the sacred," once it has been disclosed as "pure unbounded love," shall be adored in such a fashion that moral goodness, righteous concern, and intelligent or rational thought are present as qualifications. The basic attitude of worship remains, however, as the response of the total human agent—body, mind, will, emotion, and everything else that contributes to wholeness—to that which, or to him who, is thus disclosed as sheer goodness or excellence.

In the second place, Whitehead's well-known dictum about religion as moving from God as "the void," through God as "the enemy," to God as "the companion," must have its place in this context. While his intention was to speak historically—and there is much which confirms his analysis in this respect—we may take this dictum as also understandable in an experiential way. The initial and vague sense of "the sacred," which indeed resembles a "void," can become to any responsible man or woman an "enemy" when that person grasps the sheer "rightness" which runs through the world and hence knows his own unworthiness— as Whitehead himself pointed out. When "the sacred" is known as Love, such as the "Galilean vision" discloses, there emerges the deep sense of "companionship" along with experienced "refreshment." These for Whitehead were essential elements in valid religious experience and became central in the picture. But God as "companion" is not to be presumed upon or toyed with. This is why Whitehead rejected the sentimentality which much nineteenth-century liberalism substituted for rigorous thought. There is all the difference in the world between genuine sentiment and responsive emotion, on the one hand, and sentimentality or emotionalism, on the other. For the latter Whitehead had only contempt.

Third, Whitehead carefully balanced personal religion and religion in its social expression. His famous statement that "religion is what the individual does with his solitariness," coupled with his remark that a person "who is never solitary is never religious," has frequently been sadly misunderstood. He was not denying the social quality of religious experience, for in the Whiteheadian view this would be impossible in any case since to be an "actual entity" *is* to be a social participant. There is no possibility for "rugged individualism," in Herbert Hoover's unhappy phrase, in the Whiteheadian metaphysic. It is indeed true that without "solitariness," by which he plainly meant awareness of personal integrity and the sense of responsibility attaching to each self, there can be no profound religious awareness. For him such awareness is never simply a "crowd reaction." Yet it is equally true that each person relates himself or herself to a community of faith; and a person should do this on a high level of moral and rational, as well as emotional, self-awareness and self-criticism, just as in other areas of human experience selfhood can be given right expression only in terms of social belonging and participation. He himself says in *Religion in the Making* that "the topic of religion is individuality in community." What one *does* with his or her "solitariness," when doing the right thing religiously speaking, is to bring that selfhood, in full awareness of responsible decision and with rational understanding and moral zeal, to the cultural and social reality of religious observance and expression.

Fourth, Whitehead speaks in the same book of the close relationship of "cult" and "myth." The former provides the proper setting for the latter, which has its significance as an explanation of what the "cult" means. Both go together and "cult" is not lost once explanation or "myth" has been given. What happens is rather a translation into a new and deeper mode of understanding. Thus in Christian terms we may say that the liturgical act of worship, the Christian "cult," is given its specific meaning through the proclamation of the gospel which accompanies it— this proclamation is the statement of the Christian "myth," using that last word in its modern theological sense and not in the vulgar sense of "a fairy-tale." At the same time, the proclamation requires the liturgical act, the sacramental "cult," to provide its necessary and appropriate context. Thus the requirement of Vatican Council II, that a homily is to be given at Masses which have considerable congregations, like the Reformation desire (which the successors of the great reformers were unhappily not able to enforce) for sermon and sacrament to constitute together the chief Sunday service, has validity. Here we have "cult" *and* "myth." They are moralized and rationalized, in Whitehead's sense of these words, while full participation by the laity indicates that what is going on is indeed a manifestation of "individuality in community."

5. Whitehead's remark to Matthews about what he called Catholic "doing" evidently implies that in his view such worship conforms to our creaturely existence, fits in with the basic Christian insight, and is a means to fulfillment of the human desire to give oneself in responsive love. It is both expressive and impressive. It is *expressive* since it manifests the reality of Christian faith and is appropriate to the worshipper's urge to say an "amen" to what God is believed to have done—"determined, dared, and

done," to repeat once more Christopher Smart's splendid phrase. It is *impressive* because it is a way in which the reality of that divine "doing" may be assimilated and human potentiality realized. Whatever may be its defects, the main thing that Catholics *do* in their worship is the "right" thing. On the other hand, however, Whitehead felt that the theology which explicates this worship has often been disloyal, albeit unconsciously, to the reality in question; hence it is "wrong."

Several quite practical and concrete conclusions may now be drawn. First, we are helped to see that in authentic Christian religious practice there must be a continuing stress on the sacramental, the symbolic, and the sensuous. We may be grateful that one of the main features of contemporary liturgical revival and revision, in all parts of Christendom, is a movement in this direction. Second, it becomes clear that theology must undergo what might well be styled a radical "christianization," if that theology is to be faithful to its origin in the event of Christ and is to fulfill its given task in the Christian tradition. Here too we may be grateful that one of the dominant concerns in much contemporary theology is precisely to stress the significance of divine Love as the criterion for thinking about God. Perhaps a process theologian may say that no group of Christian thinkers in our time has been more insistent on this point than those who use the general Whiteheadian conceptuality, however it may be modified in this or that particular, as the vehicle for their rethinking of theology. This is not to imply that Whitehead's "vision of reality" is the only possible one; neither is it to talk as if one must begin with that conceptuality and then seek, somehow or other, to fit Christianity into it. In fact, one must work the other way round. The Christian tradition into which we are baptized and in which we stand, to which we belong, is our starting place. The Whiteheadian perspective assists us in getting at the heart of that tradition, helping us to emphasize the central reality of what is there known and experienced, and making it possible for us to work out a statement of the historic faith which is both "adequate to the original Christian witness and appropriate in our own day" (to put the point in some words of Schubert Ogden, the American process theologian).

What is required of us, therefore, is a continuing emphasis on the sacramental setting and nature of Christian worship and a

similar emphasis on such a theological reconstruction as shall focus on God as cosmic Lover, with human life as now being created
to become a creaturely image of that Lover. Worship must be ordered so that the total human personality is involved—and here
the use of light, color, music, appropriate language, movement,
and perhaps even the incense that Whitehead mentioned, will be
of enormous assistance. Everything that is said and done in worship must unmistakably declare that God is indeed the cosmic
Love and Lover, who in Jesus Christ acted focally in love for our
human becoming in actual fact what potentially his children are in
the divine intention: that is, creaturely lovers who dwell in love
with their brothers and sisters and hence both reflect the divine
charity and also serve gladly and freely as the personalized agents
of that charity in the world.

This on the one hand. On the other, the theology which provides "reasons" for what is done in worship must be centered in
the vision of God as himself sheer Love, whatever radical rethinking of traditional doctrinal positions this may entail. But this can
be done without disloyalty to the deepest intention of the received
Christian stream of life, for the Christian community of faith
(like every other social reality) is itself a process or movement. It
is a social process which looks to its past for its point of departure,
lives in the present where it brings that past into contact with contemporary life in all its complexity and with all its problems, and
envisages a future when more and more fully God's love will have
sway in the world and his children will be free to serve him in a just
society foreshadowing his "kingdom."

In what is done in worship, sentimentality is to be avoided, but
the need for healthy sentiment is to be recognized. In preaching,
didacticism is to be avoided, but the necessity for a reasonable
statement of faith is to be understood and accepted. In conduct,
moralism is to be avoided, but the moral imperatives of love human and Love divine are to be grasped. In personal devotion,
emotionalism is to be avoided, but the emotional quality of human response is to be made plain. Everywhere vulgar appeals to
sensuous feelings are to be avoided, but the truth that each of us is
a sensuous creature is to be accepted. When worship, or "what
Catholics do," is accompanied by a sound theology which is intent on finding its criterion in "the love of God which was in

Christ Jesus our Lord," and by action which seeks for true justice and human freedom, we are moving in the "right" direction: our reasons are "right." In both these ways we have to do with sheer Christian integrity.

If I am correct in my interpretation of Whitehead's meaning, he can be said to urge just such integrity. It is this central aspect of this theological reconception, the model which is best because it can be used to express a basically Christian understanding of God, the world, and human life, with which the present book has been concerned.

Notes

Chapter 2

1. Alfred North Whitehead, *Process and Reality* (New York: Macmillan, 1933, rev. ed., 1967; Free Press, 1969).

2. E. G. Selwyn, ed., *Essays Catholic and Critical* (London: SPCIC, and New York: Macmillan, 1926); facsimile ed. Essay Index Reprint Series (Freeport, N.Y.: Books for Libraries).

3. Perry Lefevre, ed., *Philosophical Resources for Christian Thought* (Nashville: Abingdon, 1968).

4. E. L. Mascall, *Theology and the Future* (New York: Morehouse-Barlow, 1958).

5. Gregor Smith, *The New Man* (London: SCM, 1956).

6. Gregor Smith, *Secular Christianity* (London: Collins, 1966).

7. John Macquarrie, *Principles of Christian Theologies*, 2nd ed. (New York: Scribner's 1977).

8. Norman Pittenger, *Process Thought and the Christian Faith* (New York: Macmillan, 1968; Welywyn, Herts.: Nisbet, 1969).

9. Norman Pittenger, *God in Process* (Naperville, Ill.: Allenson, 1967); revised as second part of *The Lure of Divine Love: Human Experience and Christian Faith in a Process Perspective* (New York: Pilgrim Press; Edinburgh: T. and T. Clark, 1979).

Chapter 3

1. Alfred North Whitehead, *Adventures of Ideas* (New York: Macmillan, 1933), p. 161.

2. Alfred North Whitehead, *Modes of Thought* (New York Putnam, 1958; Free Press, 1969), pp. 231–232.

3. Whitehead, *Process and Reality*, p. 47.

4. Ibid., p. 521.

5. Donald E. Sherburne, ed., *A Key to Whitehead's Process and Reality* (New York: Macmillan, 1966; Bloomington, Ind.: Indiana University Press, 1971), p. 226.

6. Whitehead, *Process and Reality*, pp. 515–520.

7. Whitehead, *Adventures of Ideas*, pp. 170–171.

8. Whitehead, *Process and Reality*, p. 532.

9. Ibid., p. 525.

10. Ibid., italics mine.

11. Ibid.

12. Ibid., p. 532.

Chapter 4

1. Alfred North Whitehead, *Religion in the Making* (New York: Macmillan, 1926; Mountain View, Cal.: World; New York: NAL).

2. Whitehead, *Process and Reality*, p. 47.

3. Whitehead, *Religion in the Making*, p. 55.

4. Ibid., pp. 56–57.

5. Ibid., p. 129.

6. Ibid., p. 31.

7. Ibid., p. 131.

8. Ibid., p. 126.

9. Ibid.

10. Ibid., p. 135, italics mine.

11. The discussion of "solitariness" is on pp. 16–19.

12. Whitehead, *Religion in the Making*, p. 132.

13. Ibid., pp. 15–17.

14. Ibid., p. 15.

15. John A. Robinson, *Honest to God* (Philadelphia: Westminster, 1963).

16. John A. Robinson, *The New Reformation* (Philadelphia: Westminster, 1965).

17. Whitehead, *Adventures in Ideas*, p. 170.

18. William Temple, *Nature, Man, and God* (London: Macmillan, 1935).

19. *Dialogues of Alfred North Whitehead*, as recorded by Lucien Price (Boston: Little, Brown, 1954; NAL, Mentor, New York: 1956), p. 296.

Chapter 5

1. Hubert Cunliffe-Jones, *Christian Theology Since 1600*, Studies in Theology Series (Naperville, Ill.: Allenson, 1970), p. 163.

2. Paul Goodman, "The New Reformation," *Sunday New York Times Magazine*, September 14, 1969, p. 155.

3. Trevor Ling, *Religions East and West* (New York: Macmillan, 1968).

Chapter 6

1. Daniel Day Williams, "Suffering and Being in Empirical Theology," in Fred Bertho et al., *The Future of Empirical Theology*, ed. Bernard Meland, Essays in Divinity Series, 7 (Chicago: University of Chicago Press, 1970), pp. 175–194.

2. Line, *Religions East and West*.

Chapter 7

1. Pierre Teilhard de Chardin, *The Phenomenon of Man*, trans. Bernard Wall (New York: Harper and Row, 1959).

2. Pierre Teilhard de Chardin, *The Divine Milieu* (New York: Harper and Row, 1960).

Chapter 8

1. John Hick, ed., *The Myth of God Incarnate* (London: SCM; Philadelphia: Westminster, 1977).

2. Michael Green, ed., *The Truth of God Incarnate* (Grand Rapids, Mich.: Eerdmans, 1977).

3. Maurice Wiles, "Myth" in *The Myth of God Incarnate,* ed. John Hicks (London: SCM; Philadelphia: Westminster, 1978), p. 163.

4. Christopher Smart, *A Song to David,* Augustan Books of Poetry, vol. 6 (London: E. Benn, 1931).

Chapter 9

1. Paul Lehmann, *Ethics in a Christian Context* (New York: Harper and Row, 1976).

2. Norman Pittenger, *The Word Incarnate* (New York: Harper and Row; Welywyn, Herts.: Nisbet, 1959), p. 188.

3. John A. Robinson, *The Human Face of God* (London: SCM, 1973), p. 199.

Chapter 10

1. Norman Pittenger, *The Christian Church as Social Process* (Philadelphia: Westminster, 1972).

Chapter 11

1. Alfred North Whitehead, *The Function of Reason* (Boston: Beacon, 1958), p. 8.

2. Norman Pittenger, *After Death: Life in God* (New York: Seabury, 1980), p. 190.

Chapter 12

1. W. R. Matthews, *Memories and Meanings* (London: Hodder and Stoughton, 1970).

2. Whitehead, *Dialogues*, p. 297.

3. Whitehead, *Process and Reality*, pp. 278–279.

4. Whitehead, *Dialogues*, p. 131.

5. Alfred North Whitehead, *Science and the Modern World* (New York: Macmillan, 1926; Free Press, 1967).

6. A. H. Johnson, *Whitehead's Philosophy of Civilization* (Boston: Beacon, 1958).

7. Donald Sherburne, "Whitehead without God," *The Christian Scholar* 50 (1967); 251–272.

Index of Persons

(Jesus Christ is not listed in this index since references to him occur on almost every page. This is also the case with Alfred North Whitehead. Topics discussed can readily be noted from chapter and page headings.)

OTHER ORBIS TITLES

ANDERSON, Gerald H.
ASIAN VOICES IN CHRISTIAN THEOLOGY

"Anderson's book is one of the best resource books on the market that deals with the contemporary status of the Christian church in Asia. After an excellent introduction, nine scholars, all well-known Christian leaders, present original papers assessing the theological situation in (and from the viewpoint of) their individual countries. After presenting a brief historical survey of the development of the Christian church in his country, each author discusses 'what is being done by the theologians there to articulate the Christian message in terms that are faithful to the biblical revelation, meaningful to their cultural traditions, and informed concerning the secular movements and ideologies.' An appendix (over 50 pages) includes confessions, creeds, constitutions of the churches in Asia. Acquaintance with these original documents is imperative for anyone interested in contemporary Asian Christian theology." *Choice*

ISBN 0-88344-017-2   *Cloth $15.00*
ISBN 0-88344-016-4   *Paper $7.95*

APPIAH-KUBI, Kofi & Sergio Torres
AFRICAN THEOLOGY EN ROUTE

Papers from the Pan-African Conference of Third World Theologians, Accra, Ghana.
"If you want to know what 17 Africans are thinking theologically today, here is the book to check." *Evangelical Missions Quarterly*
"Gives us a wonderful insight into the religious problems of Africa and therefore is well worth reading." *Best Sellers*

"This collection of presentations made at the 1977 Conference of Third World Theologians reveals not a finished product but, as the title suggests, a process. . . .On the whole, the book is well written and, where necessary, well translated. It adds to a growing literature on the subject and is recommended for libraries seriously concerned with theology in Africa." *Choice*

ISBN 0-88344-010-5   *184pp. Paper $7.95*

BALASURIYA, Tissa
THE EUCHARIST AND HUMAN LIBERATION

"Balasuriya investigates. . .the problem of why people who share the Eucharist also deprive the poor of food, capital, and employment. . . .For inclusive collections." *Library Journal*

"I hope Christians—especially Western Christians—will read this book, despite its blind impatience with historical and ecclesial details and balance, because its central thesis is the gospel truth: eucharistic celebration, like the faith it expresses, has been so domesticated by feudalism, colonialism, capitalism, racism, sexism, that its symbolic action has to penetrate many layers of heavy camouflage before it is free, before it can be felt." *Robert W. Hovda, Editorial Director, The Liturgical Conference*

ISBN 0-88344-118-7   *184pp. Paper $6.95*

BURROWS, William R.
NEW MINISTRIES: THE GLOBAL CONTEXT

"This is an exciting, informed, thoughtful, and ground-breaking book on one of the most vital and threatening issues facing the contemporary church. Father Burrows seeks effectively to show that the older forms of church and clerical life, developed in the West, are both irrelevant and stultifying when transferred *in toto* to the Third World, and that as a consequence, new forms of church and clerical life, forms still within the Catholic heritage to which he belongs and which he affirms, must be developed if the church is long to survive in that new World. Burrows makes crystal clear the need for more open attitudes towards the forms of church and clergy if the newer churches are to become genuinely creative forces in the Third World rather than lingering embassies from the First World. I found the work exceedingly stimulating and the approach fresh and open." *Prof. Langdon Gilkey, University of Chicago Divinity School*

ISBN 0-88344-329-5   *192pp. Paper $7.95*

CABESTRERO, Teofilo

FAITH: CONVERSATIONS WITH CONTEMPORARY THEOLOGIANS

"This book shows what an informed and perceptive journalist can do to make theology understandable, inviting, and demanding. These records of taped interviews with fifteen European and Latin American theologians serve two major purposes: we are allowed to eavesdrop on well-known theologians in spontaneous theological conversation, and we are introduced to new and stimulating minds in the same way."*Prof. D. Campbell Wyckoff, Princeton Theological Seminary*

Conversations include Ladislaus Boros, Georges Casalis, Joseph (José) Comblin, Enrique Dussel, Segundo Galilea, Giulio Girardi, José María González Ruiz, Gustavo Gutiérrez, Hans Küng, Jürgen Moltmann, Karl Rahner, Joseph Ratzinger, Edward Schillebeeckx, Juan Luis Segundo, Jean-Marie Tillard.

ISBN 0-88344-126-8   *208pp. Paper $7.95*

CLAVER, Bishop Francisco F., S.J.

THE STONES WILL CRY OUT
Grassroots Pastorals

"Bishop Claver is the gadfly of the Philippine Catholic hierarchy who persistently buzzes in the ears of President Fernando Marcos and all his toadies. The bishop's book is a collection of fighting pastoral letters to his congregation after martial law closed the diocesan radio station and newspaper." *Occasional Bulletin*
"His gutsy strength has made him a prophet against the repressive regime. Some of his U.S. colleagues could learn from him." *National Catholic Reporter*
ISBN 0-88344-471-2   *196pp. Paper $7.95*

COMBLIN, José

THE CHURCH AND THE NATIONAL SECURITY STATE

"The value of this book is two-fold. It leads the readers to discover the testimony of those Latin American Christians who are striving to be faithful to the gospel in the midst of a most difficult situation characterized by the militarization of society, the consequent suppression of public freedom, and violation of basic human rights. It also invites the readers from other cultural and historical contexts to seek in their own situations the inspiration for a real theology of their own." *Theology Today*
ISBN 0-88344-082-2   *256pp. Paper $8.95*

JESUS OF NAZARETH
Meditations on His Humanity

"This book is not just another pious portrait of Christ. Its deeply religious insights relate the work of Jesus as modern scholarship understands it to the ills of our contemporary world." *Review of Books and Religion*
ISBN 0-88344-239-6   *Paper $4.95*

THE MEANING OF MISSION
Jesus, Christians and the Wayfaring Church

"This is a thoughtful and thought-provoking book by a Belgian theologian and social critic, who has lived and taught in Latin America for 20 years. His rich background in evangelization, both in theory and in practice, is evident throughout his book." *Worldmission*
ISBN 0-88344-305-8   *Paper $4.95*

SENT FROM THE FATHER
Meditations on the Fourth Gospel

"In a disarmingly simple and straightforward way that mirrors the Fourth Gospel itself, Comblin leads the reader back to biblical basics and in doing so provides valuable insights for personal and community reflection on what it means to be a disciple of the Lord, to be 'sent' by him." *Sisters Today*
ISBN 0-88344-453-4   *123pp. Paper $3.95*

FABELLA, Virginia, M.M. & Sergio Torres
THE EMERGENT GOSPEL
Theology from the Underside of History

"The Emergent Gospel, I believe, is an expression of a powerful and barely noticed movement. It is the report of an ecumenical conference of 22 theologians from Africa, Asia and Latin America, along with one representative of black North America, who met in Dar es Salaam, Tanzania, in August 1976. Their objective was to chart a new course in theology, one that would reflect the view 'from the underside of history,' that is, from the perspective of the poor and marginalized peoples of the world. Precisely this massive shift in Christian consciousness is the key to the historical importance of the meeting. The majority of the essays were written by Africans, a smaller number by Asians and, surprisingly, only three by Latin Americans, who thus far have provided the leadership in theology from the developing world." *America*

ISBN 0-88344-112-8   *Cloth $12.95*

FENTON, Thomas P.
EDUCATION FOR JUSTICE: A RESOURCE MANUAL

"The completeness of the source material on the topic and the adaptability of the methodology—stressing experiential education—to groups at the high school, college, or adult levels make this manual a time and energy saving boon for most anyone having to work up a syllabus on 'justice.' This manual would be a worthwhile addition to any religion and/or social studies curriculum library." *Review for Religious*

"The resource volume is rich in ideas for a methodology of teaching Christian justice, and in identifying the problems. It is also very rich in the quality of the background readings provided. The participant's volume is a catchy workbook with many illustrations. It encourages the student (young or adult) to look at the problems as they are experienced by real live persons." *The Priest*

"Replete with background essays, tested group exercises, course outlines and annotated bibliography, this manual should give any teacher or seminar leader plenty of material to launch a thorough study program—and plenty of strongly stated positions for students to react to." *America*

ISBN 0-88344-154-3   *Resource Manual $7.95*
ISBN 0-88344-120-9   *Participant Workbook $3.95*

GUTIERREZ, Gustavo
A THEOLOGY OF LIBERATION

Selected by the reviewers of *Christian Century* as one of the twelve religious books published in the 1970s which "most deserve to survive."

"Rarely does one find such a happy fusion of gospel content and contemporary relevance." *The Lutheran Standard*

ISBN 0-88344-477-1   *Cloth $7.95*
ISBN 0-88344-478-X   *Paper $4.95*

HENNELLY, Alfred
THEOLOGIES IN CONFLICT
The Challenge of Juan Luis Segundo

"This is another, and a significant, addition to the growing literature on liberation theology. Hennelly's intent is to initiate a dialogue with Latin American theologians and thus foster an indigenous North American liberation theology. After two introductory chapters in which he situates and overviews this new movement, he focuses on Segundo's articulation of some central liberation themes: the relation between history and divine reality, the role of the church, theological method, spirituality, and the significance of Marxism. Throughout, he draws heavily on material not available in English. Hennelly does not write as a critic of but as a spokesperson for Segundo; yet his own convictions are evident when, at the end of each chapter, he extracts challenging questions for North Americans. He voices a growing awareness: the impossibility, the sinfulness, of carrying on theology detached from social-political realities. Definitely for most theology collections." *Library Journal*

"Father Hennelly provides an excellent introduction to Juan Segundo's thought and a helpful guide to the voluminous literature, presenting the theology not as 'systematic' but as 'open': methodological principles allowing for growth and development take precedence over systematic organization of concepts." *Paul Deats, Professor of Social Ethics, Boston University*

ISBN 0-88344-287-6 — *224pp. Paper $8.95*

HERZOG, Frederick
JUSTICE CHURCH

The author, Professor of Systematic Theology at Duke Divinity School, continues the pioneering work he began in *Liberation Theology* (1972). *Justice Church* presents the *first* North American methodology of liberation theology while also critically analyzing what is and what should be the function of the Church in contemporary North America.

"Herzog refuses to do an easy or obvious theology, but insists on raising difficult questions which require theology to be done with some anguish. He has seen more clearly than most that we are in a crisis of categories, which must be reshaped in shattering ways." *Walter Brueggemann, Eden Theological Seminary*

"For us in Latin America, the question of how North Americans do theology is critically important. Besides its intrinsic value for the United States and Canada, this book should stimulate theological conversation across the North-South divide." *Jose Miguez Bonino, Dean of the Higher Institute of Theological Studies, Buenos Aires*

ISBN 0-88344-249-3 — *176pp. Paper $6.95*

RAYAN, Samuel

THE HOLY SPIRIT

Heart of the Gospel and Christian Hope

"*The Holy Spirit* by Samuel Rayan, an important Indian theologian, gives a bold interpretation of the New Testament and of the central role of the Holy Spirit, a role which western Christianity has often neglected." *Cross Currents*

"This work has a freshness and vitality that is captivating and thought-provoking. It should be read slowly because Rayan speaks truth so simply and beautifully that I found my reading moving easily to reflection and prayer. It is a book not to be easily forgotten because it so well integrates the action of the Spirit with the call to do justice in the world. I hope it will have wide circulation since it can easily be a source for personal spiritual growth, a teaching resource for prayer communities and parish education groups, and a means of formation of Christian leaders." *Catholic Charismatic*

ISBN 0-88344-188-8 *Paper $5.95*

REILLY, Michael Collins, S.J.

SPIRITUALITY FOR MISSION

Historical, Theological, and Cultural Factors for a Present-Day Missionary Spirituality

"Reilly's thesis is that, since the nature of missionary work has changed in recent years and since the theology of mission is now in a state of development, the motivation and spirituality for the modern missionary must also change. *Spirituality for Mission* synthesizes much of the current discussion on mission work and the concerns related to missionary work. Much recent literature deals with missions, but the significance of this book is that it treats the person who is involved in missionary work. It sets forth the importance and value of the missionary vocation." *Theological Studies*

"The book is a rich one. Reilly's statements on evangelization and development, on the aims of mission, and other questions are clearer than many other statements published in recent years." *Philippine Studies*

ISBN 0-88344-464-X *Paper $8.95*